AMERICAN
HERITAGE

October, 1972 • Volume XXIII, Number 6

LETTER FROM THE EDITOR

Who are these gentlemen? Our staff, or former staff, gathered together to hand out rejection slips and, just possibly, a grudging acceptance? Alas not. They are, from left, John Greenleaf Whittier, Oliver Wendell Holmes, Ralph Waldo Emerson, John Lothrop Motley, Bronson Alcott, Nathaniel Hawthorne (looking up in apparent boredom from a manuscript), James Russell Lowell, Louis Agassiz, and Henry Wadsworth Longfellow. What a set of contributors! We break no confidence when we reveal that these literary Brahmins were never photographed together; the picture is scissors-and-paste work by the noted photographer William Notman or by someone in his Boston studio. It is one of a whole drawerful of pictures of the kind any editor collects, at least one with the habits of a squirrel; it is one of those illustrations without an article that one can't use and can't throw away, like a single sock. In similar fashion we have five presidents of Harvard sitting together, six presidents of the American Historical Association, and—on a more interesting level—a beautiful picture of Maude Adams and a hilarious portrait of Joseph Choate. Someday the other sock, the article to go with each of these pictures, may appear.

Another drawer near the pictures (it is easy to tell that we are packing) yields stranger finds—seven unidentified keys, a plaque for a forgotten and minor honor, two pen points without a holder, a pipe in the shape of an early locomotive, a small saucer marked "Votes for Women" (purportedly from the home of the late Mrs. O. H. P. Belmont, where all the crockery bore that inscription), and a set of cards for the game of Authors, bearing most of the faces shown above. And also a Willkie button, a moose call bestowed by a hearty western visitor who claimed falsely that it possessed magic powers over the feminine ear, and a Petty Girl calendar, unused, for 1947.

We are not attempting social history, merely moving from Fifth Avenue after eighteen years in one place; indeed we started out simply to announce the change until trapped by that drawer of pictures. Pulling up stakes is a sad and reflective business; it means a housecleaning. By the time our readers receive this number, we should be ensconced on the twenty-third floor of the towering new McGraw-Hill Building, part of Rockefeller Center, at 1221 Avenue of the Americas, New York 10020. (Everyone but the post office, of course, calls it Sixth Avenue.) With us go our sister magazine, HORIZON, our book operations, our business departments, the offices of our tours and other arcane operations, our very considerable library, and our picture collection of history and art, which numbers some 250,000 items and is unique in its field. Our circulation office, which handles subscriptions, remains at the same address in Marion, Ohio. Meanwhile we shall continue editing the magazine as before and strive, especially with our lofty new perspective, to attract ever better contributors—keenly aware, of course, that none of the eminent writers shown above ever saw a twenty-third floor, or even half that height, yet performed, for all that handicap, rather well. To slip into Madison Avenue argot, the name of the game in magazines is still Authors.

—*Oliver Jensen*

AMERICAN HERITAGE

The Magazine of History

SENIOR EDITOR
Bruce Catton

EDITOR
Oliver Jensen

ARTICLES EDITOR
E. M. Halliday

EXECUTIVE EDITOR
Nat Brandt

ASSOCIATE EDITORS
Barbara Klaw   Bernard A. Weisberger

ART DIRECTOR
Emma Landau

PICTURE EDITORS
Carla Davidson   Mary Dawn Earley
ASSISTANT: Devorah Kanter

COPY EDITOR
Joyce O'Connor
ASSISTANT: Anne D. Steinhardt

CONSULTING EDITOR: Joan Paterson Kerr

CONTRIBUTING EDITORS
Robert C. Alberts   Robert S. Gallagher

ADVISORY BOARD
Carl Carmer   Eric F. Goldman
Gerald Carson   Louis C. Jones
Henry Steele Commager   Alvin M. Josephy, Jr.
Marshall B. Davidson   Howard H. Peckham
John A. Garraty   Francis S. Ronalds
S. K. Stevens

AMERICAN HERITAGE PUBLISHING CO., INC.

PRESIDENT AND PUBLISHER
Paul Gottlieb

EDITOR IN CHIEF
Joseph J. Thorndike

SENIOR EDITOR
Richard M. Ketchum

EDITORIAL ART DIRECTOR
Murray Belsky

AMERICAN HERITAGE is published every two months by American Heritage Publishing Co., Inc.; editorial and executive offices, 1221 Avenue of the Americas, New York, N.Y. 10020. Treasurer, Marjorie C. Dyer; Secretary, John C. Taylor III. Correspondence about subscriptions should be sent to American Heritage Subscription Office, 383 West Center Street, Marion, Ohio 43302. Single copies: $5.00. Annual subscriptions: $20.00 in U.S. and Canada; $21.00 elsewhere.

A ten-year Index covering Volumes VI–XV is available at $5.00, and a five-year Index of Volumes XVI–XX at $3.50.

AMERICAN HERITAGE will consider but assumes no responsibility for unsolicited materials. Title registered U.S. Patent Office. Second-class postage paid at New York, N.Y., and at additional mailing offices.

Sponsored by
American Association for State & Local History · Society of American Historians

CONTENTS *October, 1972 · Volume XXIII, Number 6*

COVER: George Caleb Bingham (1811–1879) was a superb painter of genre, and he devoted most of his career to living in and recording the life of Missouri, then still very much a part of the frontier. Its rugged democracy comes through in this painting, *The County Election*, which we reproduce through the courtesy of The Boatmen's National Bank, of St. Louis; it is one of seven paintings Bingham made of elections—not lampoons but accurate pictures of the crowds and scenes of rural politics, where everyone from the town drunk to the judge was equal, at least when he dropped his ballot into the box. The scene has, in a way, much in common with our electoral process today.

A DEARTH OF HEROES

By ROBERT PENN WARREN

In America the status of hero—durable, full-fledged hero—has been awarded to few men. The subtle, complex factors that have led us to be so selective were brilliantly described three decades ago in a book, The Hero in America, *by historian Dixon Wecter. For a reissue of this book, which will be published later this month by Charles Scribner's Sons, novelist and poet Robert Penn Warren has written an introduction examining Mr. Wecter's categories for glorification and speculating about who today—in this present age of the "Anti-Hero" or the "Slob-as-Hero"—might be candidates for future canonization.* AMERICAN HERITAGE *is proud to publish Mr. Warren's thoughtful and witty introduction to this classic work of history.*

Dixon Wecter's *Hero in America* appeared in 1941, on the eve of our entry into World War II, but now, three decades later, no book could be more relevant—more disturbingly relevant—to our national condition. In 1941 the "heroes" Mussolini and Hitler (along with their brother-hero Stalin, who happened to wind up on our side) dominated Europe and, as though with the morning sun of a new world-day at the back, cast their enormous shadows across the Atlantic. Could we produce a brand of heroism to stand against the apparently invincible, and inevitable, European product?

So this "Chronicle of Hero-Worship," as it is called in the subtitle, assessed the heroes of the American past in a context that gave the subject more than academic interest. It was, we may say without much exaggeration, a subject involving life and death. And now, in a time that among other things is an age of anti-heroism, as America faces a crisis which is deeper, more inward and more dire because more inward, and for which no happy issue is guaranteed, we may again say, with even less exaggeration, that this book treats a subject still involving the life and death of our society.

It is very strange that nobody before Dixon Wecter had ever undertaken such a book as *The Hero in America*. This, however, is what we always say about even—about especially—the most original and important books after they have appeared. Once written they always seem so obvious and inevitable. As Emerson put it, we recognize in them our own rejected ideas. Wecter's book, though it appeared at a crucial time in our history, would have seemed obvious and inevitable, and important, at any time. Its importance depends, primarily, on its basic conception. It is one of those studies—like "The Significance of the Frontier in American History" by Frederick Jackson Turner, *Virgin Land* by Henry Nash Smith, or *Patriotic Gore* by Edmund Wilson—that by viewing our history from the angle of vision provided by a particular topic shifts everything into new perspectives and relations, opens new vistas, and casts new shadows: new shadows because by investigating our history in relation to the new topic, we not only discover new truths but find that old truths are no longer true and that we must confront new mysteries. We thought we knew all about Washington, Benjamin Franklin, John Brown, Robert E. Lee, Buffalo Bill, and Thomas A. Edison, but once we set them side by side on the table and inspect them, we must ask what common denominator of the heroic we find—or do not find.

In this inspection, which leads not only into by-paths and covered ways of history but into strange recesses of ethical analysis and psychological speculation, we find not only fresh acquaintance with the heroes, the hero-makers, and the hero-worshippers, but unexpected confrontations with ourselves. For if the hero is the embodiment of our ideals, the fulfillment of our secret needs, and the image of the daydream self, then to analyze him is likely to mean an analysis of ourselves. By a man's hero ye shall know him. So we may come to know ourselves even better than we had ever wanted to.

To create a hero is, indeed, to create a self, and that is why, as Wecter points out, colonial societies—Canada, for instance, in spite of its vast spaces, long history, and bustling life—have no heroes in the full sense of the word. A colonial society may, of course, have its quota of heroic figures; but their function is strictly limited, often more limited than that of the hero of a subculture within a national culture. The hero developed in a subculture may well embody aspects of what we may call the heroic potential in a national culture. For instance, the subculture of the Western Plains could provide, in Buffalo

Our heroes change with the perspective of time. Abraham Lincoln, enshrined in the Lincoln Memorial in Washington, was by no means universally beloved in his own day.
WASHINGTON CONVENTION AND VISITORS BUREAU

IN THIS TEMPLE
AS IN THE HEARTS OF THE PEOPLE
FOR WHOM HE SAVED THE UNION
THE MEMORY OF ABRAHAM LINCOLN
IS ENSHRINED FOREVER

Bill, a national hero. And that mythical "steel-drivin' man," John Henry, who died in a contest with a machine, though invented in a black culture, found at least some resonance in the soul of white America. White Americans knew something, too, about the man versus the machine.

To return to the matter of colonial society, the colonial society cannot, quite literally, call its soul its own. Furthermore, insofar as it has heroes at all, it has them on borrowed time —that is, on time borrowed from the future when it may cease to be colonial and achieve its own identity, its own soul. The point is that without the context of the communal soul, there can be no true hero—only heroic individuals.

To state the matter more precisely, the hero does not merely express a pre-existing soul, is not merely a projection of that soul; the hero belongs primarily to the process whereby the soul emerges, or to the time of testing, reaffirmation, or redefinition of the soul. The myth of the hero, in its higher reaches, is, then, that of the light-bringer, the leader out of the wilderness, the founder of cities, the breaker of horses, the slayer of dragons, the redeemer, the Hanged God, the restorer of fertility. Such a myth and such a hero may appear prematurely—that is, before the full meaning is discernible. In that case, the meaning of the myth is later recognized and the hero later hailed as a dynamic force in creating the social context in which the myth has finally been able to flower in its fullness— and with a new and more appropriate hero.

Let us, for example, take the case of Nathaniel Bacon, who in 1676 led, against the royal governor of Virginia, the rebellion known by his name. By this abortive rebellion Bacon set a pattern that was to find significant repetition precisely a century later, but it was not until 1804, by no less a person than Thomas

Jefferson, then President, that his name was salvaged from "infamy" as a "rebel" and proclaimed that of a "hero" and a "patriot." Heroic Bacon no doubt was, but of what *patria* did Jefferson regard him as a "patriot"? Fresh from England, Bacon had, in fact, scarcely set foot on Virginia soil when he was embroiled in the troubles of the colony, and he was dead, by poison or fever, inside of a year. The only answer to our question is that Jefferson, anachronistically, regarded Bacon as the patriot of a *patria* that did not come into existence until 1776 and in Bacon's time had not even been imaginable.

"The land was ours before we were the land's," as Robert Frost puts it, and the process by which we became the land's was long, complex, and arduous. No doubt, as John Adams said, the Revolution took place in the hearts of the American people years before a shot was fired, but a number of shots had to be fired on both sides and some had to dew the land with American blood before we belonged to it. Once that had occurred, the *patria* for patriots existed, and as with Bacon, so with Captain John Smith, Pocahontas, Miles Standish, and all the other early figures now safely ensconced in our national pantheon; their naturalization papers and certificates of heroism were issued quite late—often quite late indeed, Miles Standish not getting his until 1858, from Longfellow. The candidates couldn't get their papers until there was a *patria* whose values the heroes might, retroactively, be discovered to embody.

On the time when the land was finally being baptized with the redefining blood and the full flowering of the hero could occur, Wecter is especially good. Franklin, Washington, and Jefferson are the Founding Fathers who early became national heroes, and in that capacity did as much as by any services in the field or in the council to make the new

nation possible at all. It is this fact that, apparently, leads Wecter to argue that the hero has had a very special role in America, a role not known elsewhere, at least not to the same degree. If, as Wecter says, patriotism traditionally springs from love of place, then America is in a peculiar situation. To begin with, the nation was founded in terms of an idea, and as late as the 1850's the Polish political writer Adam Gurowski, in an astute book on America, distinguished the United States from all other nations on this basis. The abstract idea might be noble and our distinction might be applauded, but it was abstract; it did not immediately and firmly grip the guts.

Furthermore, from early days distance beckoned the man on this continent, and often he had scarcely learned his way around in one Eden, much less taken root there, before word came of another one, newer, brighter, and more felicitous, farther upriver or over the mountains. Even in early times, distance was a potent factor in making Americans out of displaced Europeans; and once Americans were made, especially after Jefferson had set the flag on the Pacific—against all his political principles as well as his agrarian sense of locality—the dream of distance, like the dream of the future, fed the national ego. These twin dreams were fundamentally dynamic for our very existence, but they drained off the vital blood from more specific attachments to a particular place and to a particular past. The dreams did give a sense of grandeur and an air of confidence to Americans, but they also meant that American life often exhibited that thin, abstract quality later noted by George Santayana.

That same abstractness was early to be remarked even in American patriotism, as by the traveller Francis Grund, who, in 1838, observed that an "American's country is in his understanding; he carries it with him wherever he goes." In New England and parts of the South, though both sections provided their quotas of westward wayfarers and Eden-seekers, patriotism of the traditional sort did persist; but the *patria* was usually quite local. Even at the time of the Civil War, when the Union was being saved, Hawthorne, for instance, could say that his affections did not easily reach beyond the boundaries of New England; and Lee famously gave Virginia first rank in his loyalties. The baptism of blood, the shared effort of the struggle to save the Union, and the mobility dictated by the war, reaffirmed for Northerners the national patriotism—just as for Southerners it created the "South" as a City of the Soul, an entity now safely beyond characteristic internal dissension and historical accident; but the new American patriotism, with the transcontinental railroads, the explosion of population westward, the movement toward urban centralization, and the rise of finance capitalism and big industry, became, not less, but more abstract than the older variety. Whitman grasped this fact when, in "Song of the Banner at Daybreak," he hymned the flag as "an idea only"—the pure idea into which all might be absorbed, the abstraction in which all distinctions are wiped away:

> *Valueless, object of eyes,*
> *over all and demanding all—*
> *(absolute owner of all)—*
> *O banner and pennant!*
> *I too leave the rest—great as*
> *it is, it is nothing—houses,*
> *machines are nothing, I see*
> *them not,*
> *I see but you, O warlike pen-*
> *nant! O banner so broad, with*
> *stripes, I sing you only,*
> *Flapping up there in the wind.*

The flag gave at least some sort of concrete focus for the abstract emotion, but, as again Whitman instinctively recognized, Lincoln, struck down at the moment of victory and thus redeemed from the sneer and

snarl of political action, constituted an even more potent symbol. And this returns us to Wecter's point. In our world of mobility and abstraction, heroes along with our other "collective symbols," such as the flag, the Declaration of Independence, and the Constitution, are more precious to us than the corresponding elements in the life of other countries in that they "nourish our sense of national continuity." Our brand of hero worship, then, resembles—or did resemble—the worship in a religion, with shrines, high places, relics, fetishes, holy books, and saints—saints especially, for we have to disinfect our heroes from all mortal frailty.

As for the Founding Fathers, Wecter sees in the trio who became our first national heroes a fascinating projection of the various, even paradoxical, aspects of the American soul. What Franklin represents is the most obvious and simple of all, and we should not be misled by President Coolidge's tribute read at the unveiling of the hero's statue in the Hall of Fame in 1927: "Franklin is claimed by more groups than any other person in our history." The groups that claim Franklin are indeed numerous, including the Rotary Club (Franklin's club in Philadelphia, the Junto, being regarded as the first "service" organization); investment bankers (because Franklin preached thrift, even if he did habitually overdraw his account); prohibitionists (only by very careful culling of evidence); printers (Franklin made his fortune in printing but retired from business at the age of forty to devote himself to study and public service); and organized labor (being hailed by William Green of the A.F. of L. as the "Patron Saint of Labor"); and he might well be claimed, too, by public utility companies on the strength of his experiments with electricity. The groups that claim Franklin are numerous, surely, but they are not at

bottom various; they are all part and parcel of bourgeois democracy—even organized labor, which aspires to the same consumer goods and mass amusements as the most well-heeled Rotarian.

Franklin is, in fact, the perfect hero of a bourgeois democracy, the very model of the Industrious Apprentice who, by pluck (not luck), thrift, self-denial, temperance, prudence, and a streak of hard, realistic calculation (not often mentioned), rises, without social, financial, or intellectual advantages, to high solvency and world fame. But Franklin embodied not only the universal bourgeois virtues, but also some special American ones. He had, for instance, a truly democratic spirit of tolerance (far ahead of his time, and ours), and he represented in full flower the American passion for gadgetry, being the inventor of, among other things, bifocal glasses, the lightning rod, and the stove known by his name; and more American still, if he was learned in science, he did not get bemused by airy speculations but sternly put science to work. And through everything he remained the plain man—but the plain man who, without fuss or feathers, wearing his old fur cap, put kings in their places and was adored by duchesses, and then went on to tell everybody else how to get ahead, too. He was the Alger hero in the flesh, long before poor Horatio, that failure in life, held up his private daydream of success as a mirror to the great public daydream of America.

I have dwelt here on Franklin because of a peculiar and ironic fact; if he does seem to be the perfect hero for our bourgeois democracy, sprung in full bloom in the heroic age of the founding, he was never quite a hero of the very first rank. Perhaps he is, after all, too perfectly the projection of our personal daydreams of worldly success. Perhaps he is too close to us. Perhaps what he stands for is, after

CONTINUED ON PAGE 95

7

CAMPAIGN BANNERS

Their homely symbols

tell us more about voter

behavior than

party platforms do

By WILCOMB E. WASHBURN

Director
American Studies Program
Smithsonian Institution

Beneath the gaudy exterior and hoopla of American political parades of the nineteenth century is concealed a sober truth about ourselves. The banners used in such parades were designed to convert onlookers to a new political faith or to reinforce existing beliefs. While one school of American historians dismisses such material as the mere claptrap of political rhetoric in this country, others see the banners as providing greater insights into the psychological springs of voter behavior than do the party platforms or newspaper editorials traditionally interpreted by intellectuals as the substance of campaign debate. The fact is that yesterday's mass electorate could probably understand the complex issues of past generations no better than contemporary voters can comprehend complex issues today. Recently, scholars have attempted to understand past voter behavior by careful analysis of ethnic, religious, party, and class differences rather than by studying campaign arguments.

A glance at the banners in the following section tells us something about what kind of image of their candidate campaign managers wished to project to the people. While the sample is not scientifically selected, it tends to reflect the prevailing themes of nineteenth-century campaign banners. There are frequent graphic representations of the candidate himself or of his name and that of his running mate. Symbols range from the traditional American flag, shield, and eagle to the honest farmer behind his plow and the humble log cabin. The banners contain few words, and if they are related to issues, they are hard-hitting and precise. Party references are virtually absent.

Unlike the banners used in parades marking the ratification of the Constitution in 1788, those shown here employ no abstract symbols, like the ship of the union and the temple of liberty with its columns representing the ratifying states. These have given way to realistic objects—the log cabin, the barrel of hard cider, the plow, and the shirt-sleeved figure of a laboring farmer. As Philip Hone, a New York Whig, in commenting on the symbolism of the 1840 campaign, put it: "The American eagle has taken his flight, which is supplied by [that is, the eagle is replaced by] a cider-barrel, and the long-established emblem of the ship has given place to the plough. Hurrah for Tippecanoe! is heard more frequently than Hurrah for the Constitution! . . . [These are] weapons, the use of which is understood by every man in our ranks; who would not understand the ship, and eagle and Temple of Liberty and, whatever may be the result of this election, the hurrah is heard and felt in every part of the United States."

The results of the election of 1840 vindicated Hone, and its lessons have been studied by campaign managers since. The many advertising firms that manage campaigns at the present time are acutely conscious of the need to create forceful images and realistic symbols that are "understood by every man in our ranks." Can one not see in the banner representation of a log cabin and hard-cider barrel in 1840, and of an honest farmer behind his plow in 1860, capsule messages that might have come through a television screen if the medium had existed then? The message conveyed is the candidate's virtue and simplicity. Does the modern media-specialist do more than the maker of these banners?

The precise nature of most of the specific issues of the nineteenth century may still be read in party platforms and newspaper editorials, but those found no prominent place in the banners of the period—and they no longer remain in our memory.

A rather wooden-looking James K. Polk and his running mate George M. Dallas are sheltered by the outspread wings of a fierce American eagle in this 1844 banner, which appears to have been copied by an untutored artist from a Currier print.

JAMES K. POLK.

GEO. M. DALLAS.

The *1840 Whigs, though popular with the well-to-do, joyfully took the log cabin as a symbol of their standard-bearer's homespun virtue. In "going for" the "O.K." Harrison, the Whig carriers of this flag were early users of a brisk new synonym for "all right."*

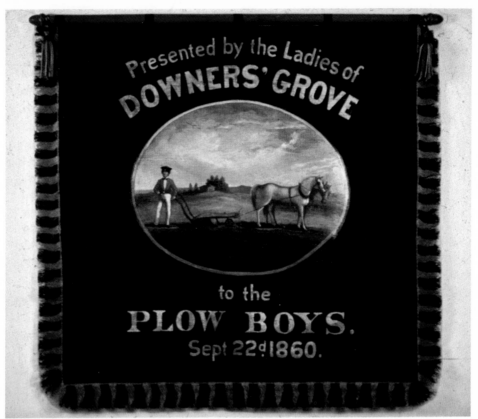

The Republican marching club of Downers' Grove bore its name proudly. "Plow Boys" were true blue.

Candidate John Frémont was a western hero, but the top slogan here, in 1856, is prosaically economic.

THE SAME OLD COON

HENRY CLAY
AND
FRELINGHUYSEN

BUCK & BRECK.

BORDER RUFFIAN

DEMOCRACY, & SLAVERY.

VICTORY IS OURS

BELFAST
WIDE AWAKE
CLUB

Above: The sly raccoon, symbol of the Whigs, is wrapped in the flag, with a campaign jingle, to win 1844 votes for canny Henry Clay.
THE HAGLEY MUSEUM, WILMINGTON, DEL.

Above: Buchanan and Brecken-ridge were Democrats; as "Buck" and "Breck," they are here lam-pooned for their proslavery stance.
NEW HAMPSHIRE HISTORICAL SOCIETY, CONCORD

Left: The shield of the United States was used by pro-Lincoln "Wide Awakes" in 1860 to pre-dict, rightly, "Victory is Ours."
DE WITT COLLECTION, UNIVERSITY OF HARTFORD

Below: Garfield and Arthur might not have known themselves in this 1880 banner, but the art form was charming though inexact.
SMITHSONIAN INSTITUTION

Opposite: A high moral tone was struck in this 1888 banner, presented by the Republican ladies of an Ohio township to their cam-paign warriors. The reversal of the clauses in Lincoln's famous quotation was evidently dictated by the shape of the banner itself.
CINCINNATI HISTORICAL SOCIETY

HARRISON AND MORTON

WITH CHARITY FOR ALL

UNION. LIBERTY.

WITH MALICE TOWARD NONE.

Reginald MARSH

A reminiscent tribute to a great American painter, with
an evocative selection from thousands of unpublished sketches

Soon after Reginald Marsh's death in 1954 an art magazine asked me to write about him. When I turned in the article the editor said he liked it but he had one reservation: "You say, 'In my opinion he was the greatest artist of his time.' Do you mean that? Greater than Picasso?"

"Yes," I answered.

When the article came out it was headed "Homage from a colleague to the chronicler of New York life on paper and canvas marks the opening of a memorial exhibition at the Whitney Museum."

At that time I felt keenly that both the magazine and the museum were there too late with too little, but time has made a tremendous difference. The fashions in art that the magazine promoted are now a bore, the museum's exhibitions of contemporary art are a bad joke, and these institutions, seventeen years after his death, have less life in them than Reginald Marsh. I have a notion (a superstition, perhaps) that artists, the real ones, live out their productive lives fully and then die when

The observer observed: self-portrait of Reginald Marsh in 1933. "Go out into the street, stare at the people," he told his students. "Stare, stare, keep on staring."

their work is done. Institutions are less graceful. They die but they won't lie down.

It was a constant pleasure to know Reginald Marsh. He was a man of extraordinary personal charm. Short and stocky, with red hair and freckles, he talked almost inaudibly out of the side of his mouth. The first time he visited my studio (this was in 1930, and we had just been introduced to each other) he spoke disparagingly of the Woodstock artists who were very big names at the time, being favored by Juliana Force, the director of the Whitney Museum in its Eighth Street days. "They vegetate up there in the country and they never make any hell!" he said, in the manner of a Dead End Kid. He left me with the disarming impression that I had been in the company of a tough little gangster. I soon learned that this manner was entirely defensive and that in reality he was a sweet, shy man of great sensibility and cultivation. He seemed somehow vulnerable, and all his friends wanted to protect him from harm.

It was a pleasure to know him and it was also a privilege. For an artist it was the sort of privilege a religious person would find in association with a saint. He was endlessly creative; he produced as Nature produces, turn-

ing out, with marvelous abundance, drawings and paintings, illustrations, etchings, engravings, and murals; and all this work was accomplished with grace and apparent ease. He was inventive; the "Marsh Girl" was an archetypal figure, and many aspects of New York life became so intimately his own that it almost seemed he had thought them up—Coney Island, the Bowery, the burlesque. He was dedicated; he was always working. After the day in his studio on Union Square was over, he walked the short distance to his apartment on Fifteenth Street and spent the evening at his etching press. And when the work in the studio faltered, he put a sketchbook in his pocket, picked up a couple of artist's fountain pens, and set out on a sketching trip. He would walk along Fourteenth Street and take the Third Avenue El to Chatham Square and the Bowery. Or in warm weather he would go to the West Side wharves and sketch the kids who dived into the Hudson and the tugboats that puffed along offshore. In bad weather he would take refuge in the burlesque theatre on Irving Place to sketch the performers and the audience. On fine summer days he would head for Coney Island.

I remember going with him to

By EDWARD LANING

15

Coney Island one day. When we got to the boardwalk he led the way to a bathhouse, where we changed into swim trunks. We picked our way over the massed bodies on the sand and went into the crowded surf. Marsh dog-paddled, his head held high above the water, while he ogled the churning arms and legs, bellies and bottoms. After that we dressed and went to "Steeplechase—The Funny Place." At the ticket booth we were waved inside without charge. (The management had left orders that Marsh was always to be admitted free.) We watched the swings and rides and chutes while Marsh made some notes in his sketchbook. Back in Manhattan we went to Sloppy Louie's restaurant for dinner, and Louie picked up the tab (Marsh had drawn Louie's portrait sketch for *The New Yorker*'s profile). Then we walked up the Bowery to Strokey's Bar—and there our drinks were on the house. (A Marsh-style painting of the Bowery, featuring Strokey's, hung on the wall behind the bartender. When we left, Reg told me the painting was a forgery. "But I don't tell them that. They want to think I did it.") Finally we took the El uptown, and we paid the full five-cent fare, though considering Marsh's celebrations of the El we should have travelled as the guests of the railway.

His sketchbooks were the central fact of his career as an artist—I almost said of his life. He always used for his drawings and water colors the best paper he could find. For his sketchbooks he carefully cut this paper to a size to fit his coat pocket. He shaped a couple of pieces of cardboard for covers, punched holes through papers and cardboard, and with metal rings made a sketchbook of fine rag paper. He had a supply of Waterman's artist's fountain pens that held India ink. I believe he never went anywhere without these sketchbooks and pens, and he drew almost incessantly.

At the time of his sudden death in

Vermont in 1954 his wife, the artist Felicia Meyer, asked me to keep an eye on his studio, across the street from my own. It was a place I was very familiar with, having visited him there on countless occasions. I found it exactly as he had intended to return to it in a few days' time. (He hated the country!) It was in that orderly disorder that is typical of artists' studios. I entered it with sadness, knowing I would never find him there again. It was a small studio but one that exactly suited his needs. On the top floor of an old commercial building at the corner of Fourteenth Street and University Place, it commanded a view of Union Square. I went to the window and looked out, remembering how Reg used to pick up his binoculars and peer out over the view, catching glimpses of the crowded streets, the great equestrian statue of Washington at the entrance to the square, S. Klein's emporium beyond, and the Consolidated Edison tower looming over all. I remembered how he would discover a group of nearly naked girls sunbathing on a roof across the square; or perhaps we would catch sight of someone run over by an automobile or truck in the street below and would watch while police cars and an ambulance hurried to the scene.

I turned back to the studio, where in his absence his easel was strangely empty. I looked up at the wall nearby and was reassured to find there that little painting which he kept as a sort of mascot—one of his girls. She had been there for years, changing constantly but ever the same, a talisman, pert and bouncy. She was one of the touchstones of his life. Every evening when it was time to go home he looked up at this little painting and brought her down to the easel for a few minutes while he reworked her with the last remaining pigments on his palette. I wonder where she is now. When I last saw her she was many inches thick!

This little studio contained his workroom (the easel occupied most of it). First, an entrance area with chests of drawers and filing cabinets. From this a narrow stairway led to the small gallery on the roof that he used mainly for the storage of paintings, hundreds of paintings in cabinets behind wooden doors. These doors were plastered with the black-bordered death notices that the National Academy of Design sends out to its members.

Returning to the filing cabinets below, I looked into them. One big architect's file contained his wash drawings on "elephant" and "double-elephant" Whatman papers. One after another I held in my hands big drawings of all his favorite subjects, almost always with another great drawing on the other side of the sheet. Then I turned to the cabinets where his pocket sketchbooks were filed and began to look through them.

I discovered that he had filed this series of sketchbooks in strict chronological order over the years, beginning in the early 1920's and continuing until his death. I had thought I knew them well, but I realized I had taken them for granted and that they were far richer than I had supposed, much as I had always admired them. I had thought I knew *him*, but here I found him as he had known himself. I spent the following days poring over these sketchbooks, beginning with the early pencil drawings and watching the development of the pen-and-ink line that became his supreme medium. I sat with him in the sidewalk cafés of Paris, met Mahonri Young and Llewelyn Powys and John Rothenstein, went to the Folies-Bergère and the Cirque d'Hiver, and strolled along the Seine. I returned with him to New York and the beginnings of his favorite subjects, the burlesque and the speakeasies of the late twenties. In these pages I met his friends and acquaintances, went with him to the theatre and to par-

TEXT CONTINUES ON PAGE 33

The World of Reginald MARSH

Reginald Marsh carried his sketchbook in his pocket everywhere he went, and with an artist's fountain pen he made sketches of everything he saw. These sketchbooks, scores of them, he filed in chronological order, often referring to them for data for his paintings. In these hitherto unpublished drawings we accompany him on his daily rounds, walking the sidewalks of New York, taking the subway to Coney Island, watching the burlesque shows, or exploring the harbor by tugboat or ferry. This remarkable record, amounting to thousands of sketches, continues from its modest but probing beginnings in the twenties to the fluent mastery of his last years—surely one of the most extraordinary pictorial diaries ever kept by an artist. The drawing at right is of a lamppost on Union Square (Marsh's studio was on the top floor of the building in the background). This was the famous "bishop's-crook" lamppost that was erected in the streets of New York in the 1890's. By 1954, when Marsh made this drawing, the lamppost was carrying a lot more than its original burden of lamp and street signs. It was now hung with traffic lights and symbols, route numbers and mailboxes. It was New York's totem pole. But it still wore an air of urban elegance, which Marsh delineated with the same loving care he devoted to the lines of a ship or the intricate structure of the El.

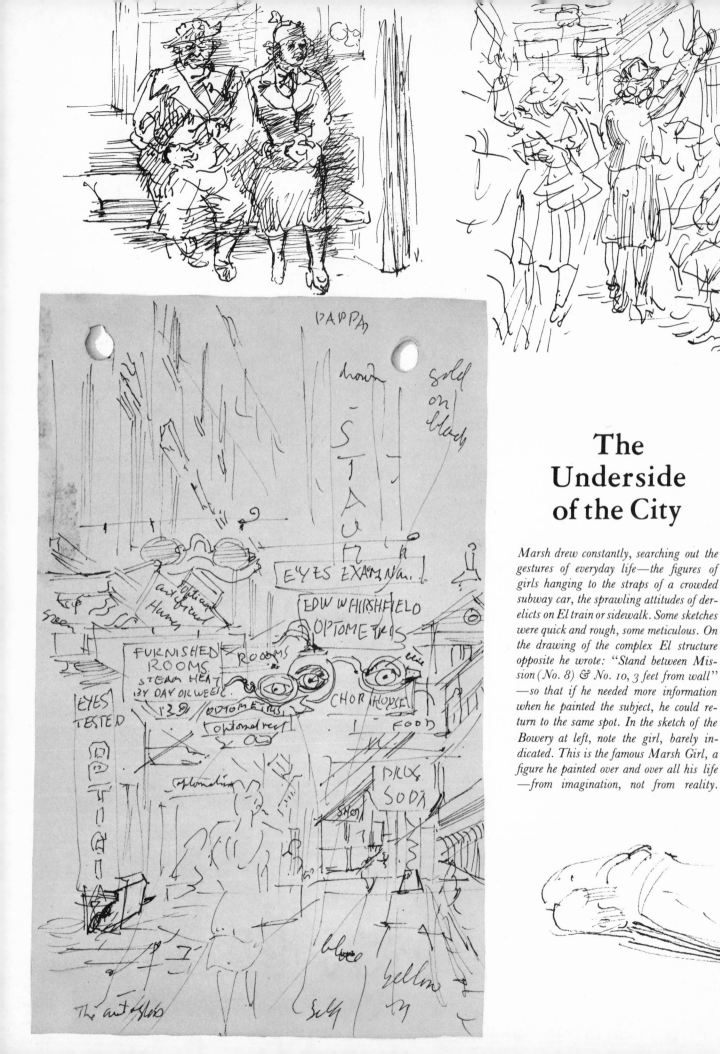

The Underside of the City

Marsh drew constantly, searching out the gestures of everyday life—the figures of girls hanging to the straps of a crowded subway car, the sprawling attitudes of derelicts on El train or sidewalk. Some sketches were quick and rough, some meticulous. On the drawing of the complex El structure opposite he wrote: "Stand between Mission (No. 8) & No. 10, 3 feet from wall" —so that if he needed more information when he painted the subject, he could return to the same spot. In the sketch of the Bowery at left, note the girl, barely indicated. This is the famous Marsh Girl, a figure he painted over and over all his life —from imagination, not from reality.

stand between No 8 & No 10 - 3 feet from wall

The Proletarian Beach

Of Coney Island Marsh said, "I've been going out there every summer, sometimes three or four days a week. On the first trip each summer I'm nauseated by the smell of stale food, but after that I get so I don't notice it. I like to go there because of the sea, the open air, and the crowds—crowds of people in all directions, in all positions, without clothing, moving—like the compositions of Michelangelo and Rubens!" Here are samples of his hundreds of Coney Island sketches.

sketched from life -
Coney Island Beach -
August 1952 -

posed for by a weight
lifter and his lady
friend - in 5 mins

medium -
   waterman's
      artist pen - filled
      with Higgins
      "engrossing ink

paper "Marilla" -

I carry these books
in the pocket every
day + pen
         Reginald Marsh

weight lifters pose readily - in exchange for sketches — Many men will pose eagerly if a girl can be induced in a desirable place

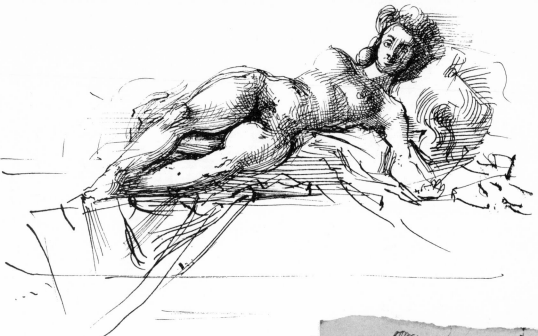

Anatomy Lessons

Marsh's absorption in the human spectacle of Coney Island, the massed bodies on the beach there, the figures on the swings and rides, led him into an intensive study of anatomy. He copied the drawings of Michelangelo, Leonardo, and Rubens and the plates in the classical anatomy books, and soon he was drawing not only what he saw but what he knew. And his comments, as on the opposite page, were often shrewd.

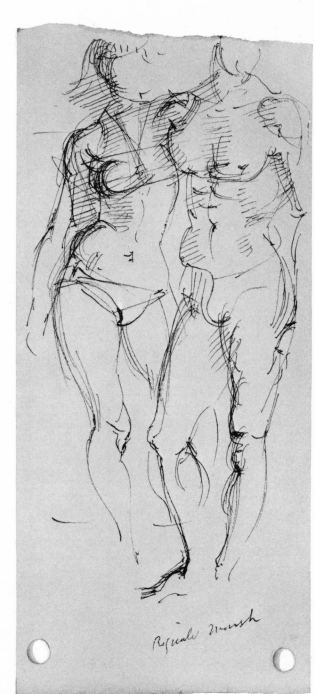

The Gathering Place

Bars are a recurring motif in Marsh's sketches. He was of that Hemingway-Fitzgerald generation that learned to drink in speakeasies. They didn't drink much, but they drank on principle. For Marsh, bars were simply a place where people held relatively still.

The Raffish Days of Burlesque

Marsh made thousands of sketches in burlesque theatres, from notes on the gilded interiors to the postures of the striptease girls, the comedians, the musicians, and the audience. He sketched clowns from the days of Grock and the Fratellini at the Cirque d'Hiver to Jimmy Savo on Forty-second Street; the girls from Dolly Dawson and Georgia Sothern to Gypsy Rose Lee. And when he was forbidden to sketch openly he drew inside his pocket, as in the sketches at the bottom of the opposite page.

People Observed

A bread line in the thirties, a sidewalk shoeshine, stompin' at Harlem's Savoy Ballroom, a Paris brothel, the Staten Island ferry—Marsh sketched endlessly; and while his observation was always quick and telling, his line became more and more fluent and incisive with the years. Pencil and crayon gave way to pen and ink; an early impression became a master's command of contour and form.

OVERLEAF: *Marsh loved New York Harbor and its ships, especially the powerful little tugs that move the heavy barges and nudge the big ships into their berths. He knew the crews of many of these tugs and often accompanied them on their voyages. Here he is aboard the ferryboat* Buffalo, *crossing to New Jersey.*

7.   The Buffalo "D.L.W

The Gateway

When he was preparing to paint the murals in the customs house at Bowling Green, Marsh frequently went out to meet incoming ocean liners, climbing aboard with reporters and quarantine examiners. He sketched the harbor's activity from Governors Island and the Statue of Liberty. The tugs sketched here are towing the Italian liner Rex *to its berth in the Hudson River.*

WE ARE GRATEFUL TO MRS. REGINALD MARSH
AND THE FRANK REHN GALLERY OF NEW YORK
FOR THEIR COURTESY IN MAKING AVAILABLE THE
MARSH SELF-PORTRAIT AND SKETCHES SHOWN HERE.

ties (he said to me one day, "When I feel neglected at a party, I reach for my sketchbook and soon everybody is gathered around, watching me draw!"), sat beside him in the subway and the El and on the Staten Island ferry, walked along Fourteenth Street and the Bowery, explored the railroad yards and the waterfront. It was a pictorial diary such as no other artist, I believe, has left behind him, at least not over such a period of time.

Marsh was born in Paris in 1898 in an apartment above the Café du Dôme. His parents were both artists, his father a successful mural painter and his mother a miniaturist. There was plenty of money (Grandfather Marsh had been a rich Chicago packer), and Alice Randall and Fred Dana Marsh were living the life of genteel expatriates. Back in America, Reginald grew up in Nutley, New Jersey, and New Rochelle, New York. He attended the Lawrenceville School and Yale. This background was quintessential New York, but upper-class New York, not the New York of the slums and the ghettos. Of another Yale man, Cole Porter, a biographer has written, "Like any Keys man, he had a certain curiosity about the gutter," and so did Marsh. He once told me that when he was a boy leading a sheltered life in a big house in New Jersey, he used to stand in the windows, looking down the long slope of the lawn toward the distant railroad line. There at the bottom of the yard on summer days hoboes would be sprawled out on the grass. Reg would look out from his windows at these tramps, wondering what sort of men they were and what lives they led. I think he went on wondering all his life.

At Yale, Marsh drew for the *Yale Record*. Lloyd Goodrich, a friend of Marsh from the days of their boyhood in New Jersey and the author of a new book about him, says that the Marsh Girl made the *Yale Record* the most successful college journal in America. Its editor, William Benton, later Undersecretary of State and senator from Connecticut, made Reg the art editor in 1920, during Marsh's senior year. Benton remained a friend and patron throughout Marsh's lifetime.

After graduation from Yale, Marsh came to New York and began to draw for newspapers and magazines. The new tabloid paper, the *Daily News*, paid him a thousand dollars a month, and from 1922 to 1925 he had a column of sketches in that paper in which he depicted vaudeville and theatre acts and nightclub turns, and gave each performance a percentage rating. When *The New Yorker* was started in 1925, Marsh began drawing for it in its second issue and was actively connected with the magazine through 1931. One day during this period Frank Crowninshield asked him if he would go out to Coney Island and make a page of sketches for *Vanity Fair*. Marsh later told me this was the first time he ever visited the place. Throughout his career he made many illustrations for other periodicals, including *Life*, *Fortune*, and *Esquire*, and for many books, such as Defoe's *Moll Flanders*, Dreiser's *Sister Carrie*, and Dos Passos' *U.S.A.* He designed theatre curtains for John Murray Anderson's *Greenwich Village Follies* and collaborated with Robert Edmond Jones on sets for *Fashion, or Life in New York*.

In his early work for the *Yale Record* and the *Daily News*, Marsh was influenced by Edmund Duffy, who was his roommate at Yale and whose later cartoons for the Baltimore *Sun* he greatly admired. All his life he studied the drawings of great English illustrators like Cruikshank and Tenniel. This background in illustration resembled that of John Sloan and other members of "The Eight," the so-called Ashcan School, many of whom began their careers as illustrators in Philadelphia, and it was in the American tradition. Winslow Homer, for example, was an "artist-correspondent" for *Harper's Weekly* during the Civil War, before he ever began to paint.

Marsh's concern with illustration involved him in the whole tradition of Western art. He knew that Giotto and Michelangelo had illustrated the Bible, that the artists of the Renaissance had taken their themes from Ovid, that Delacroix had derived his from Shakespeare. By adhering steadily to representation, Marsh was able to concentrate on what his work was about, on its story. For reasons that were essentially political, this concern with story and illustration became unfashionable in Marsh's time. The disillusionments of the Hitler-Stalin pact of 1939 led many artists to shun every form of "subject matter" and to adopt "abstract" styles. These artists said, in effect, that their commitment to the cause of revolution had been betrayed, and since they no longer had any subject, they would learn to do without; they would henceforth restrict themselves to the manipulation of their medium, to Hans Hofmann's "push and pull on the picture surface."

I think Marsh was saved from this fate by a combination of circumstances. He was never political; he was intelligent, but he was never "intellectual." He lived by his art, and his art had roots that reached back to a period earlier than universal compulsory education, to a time when the metaphor of art had to be acted out, not merely verbalized. This always meant a degree of vulgarity in his work, and it was a saving vulgarity. While many of his contemporaries sought refuge in the abstract, Marsh remained content to be entertaining. It is ironic that Marsh, who was willing humbly to illustrate words and tell stories, ultimately transcended the mere word and created a logos, while his contemporaries, many of them, ended as illustrators of the works of critics like Clement Greenberg and Harold Rosenberg (as Mr. Rosenberg has been the first to admit). And no matter that these critical exercises were by their nature unillustratable and that the "abstract" canvas became more and more blank.

Tradition was easy for Marsh to come by. Not only were his parents both painters; his first wife was a sculptor and the daughter of artists (her father was curator of painting at the Metropolitan Museum). His second wife, herself a painter, was the daughter of painters. A recent biographical account correctly states: "He lived in New York, spending week-ends in Dorset, Vermont, almost every summer, and winter vacations visiting his father at Ormond Beach, Florida, where he painted watercolors." But the tradition Marsh embraced was not the Genteel Tradition!

It is easy to say of any great artist that he did it all himself, and in America we are taught that this *must* be so. Marsh's achievement was his own, of course, but he readily acknowledged what he owed to others. He was the most independent of men, but he was also the most persistent student. He never stopped studying, never regarded his knowledge as adequate, never ceased to *wonder*. I remember going to his studio one day and being introduced by him to a stranger. They were poring over bits of calligraphy—and dollar bills! Reg had found the man on Fourteenth Street, selling examples of penmanship (for a quarter he would write the purchaser's name in fine italic script on a card). Reg had watched for a while and then said to him, "Where did you learn to use your pen like that?" The man replied, "I used to be an engraver at the mint in Washington." Reg invited him to come up to his studio and immediately began to pay him for lessons in engraving.

His periods of study at the Art Students League were inevitable. (Where else, now or then, could an artist study?) But while brief periods

with Sloan or George Luks were no more than extensions of his own predilections, his study with Kenneth Hayes Miller was critical. I am sure that it was partly his genteel relatives who impelled Marsh toward Miller's class at the League. But it was also much more. Miller was the Academy of his time, and not to have submitted oneself to Miller's examination was not to have gone through the mill. And Miller was of inestimable value to Marsh. He resolved at a glance the problem of gentility. He looked at Reg's early, awkward burlesque sketches and at his more conventional landscape water colors and said, "These awkward things are your work. These are real. Stick to these things and don't let anyone dissuade you!" In 1944 Marsh wrote, "I still show him every picture I paint. I am a Miller student."

Renoir said, "The only thing worthwhile for a painter is to study the museums," and William Benton reports that Marsh told him he had copied every great painting in Europe. In the sketchbooks there are scores of drawings after the great works of the Renaissance and baroque masters: Titian, Tintoretto, Veronese, Rubens, and Delacroix. On one of his tours of the European galleries he met Thomas Hart Benton, another great student of the baroque masters and a man who was as fluent with words as Marsh was tongue-tied. From Venice, Reg wrote a post card to Stewart Klonis: "Yesterday we ran into Tom and Rita Benton and today Tom and I went to the Scuola San Rocco. I never realized till now how much Tintoretto owed to Tom Benton!"

When an admirer said to Delacroix, "Master, you are the Victor Hugo of painting," Delacroix replied, "You don't know what you're talking about. I am a classicist, pure and simple." Marsh would have said the same thing. Believing that the

proper study of mankind is man, he decided that he needed to know more about anatomy. He arranged to take lessons at New York Hospital in the Cornell Medical School. This involved the dissection of cadavers. I asked him if he had learned anything from this. "No," he said, "nothing at all. The only way an artist can study the subject is in the best anatomical plates in the best books. I asked them at the hospital who, in New York, knows more about anatomy than anybody else and they said it's old Doctor So-and-so but he retired years ago. I asked where I could find him and they said, 'Well, he spends every day in the library.' I went there and I found him and I said, 'What are the best anatomical plates and diagrams, the best anatomical books?' The old man said, 'Vesalius.' "

Marsh began to draw from these earliest of all anatomical plates and from the drawings of masters like Raphael, Leonardo, and Michelangelo, and to relate these to each other. Around this time I acquired a whole skeleton from the Cooper Union, where my wife was a supervisor in the museum. It was nothing but a disassembled bag of bones. I told Reg about it and said I didn't think I would ever do anything with this treasure. He came at once to my studio (then on Bleecker Street), threw the gunny sack over his shoulder, and started off to Fourteenth Street, half a mile away. Until he called to tell us he was safely home we held our breath. What if he had met with an accident and the bones had been scattered over the street?

Marsh's sketching was never a mindless copying of light and shade but a penetrating examination into the structure and form of figures and objects. One day in the early years of the Second World War he took the Staten Island ferry and was soon busy drawing the ships in the crowded harbor. Suddenly two men appeared and sat down, one at either side of him. "What do you think you're do-

ing?'' they said. "Come with us.''
They took his sketchbook from him,
and at Staten Island they transferred
to the ferry to Brooklyn, where they
made their way to FBI headquarters.
At the entrance they told him to wait
on a bench while they took his sketchbook to an inner office. While he
waited he reached into his pocket for
a spare sketchbook and began to
draw from memory the ships he had
seen in the harbor. Finally the agents
returned. They looked at what he
was doing. His sketches from memory were as vivid and detailed as the
original drawings. "Oh, go away!''
the FBI men said to him. "There's
nothing we can do with you!''

Studying his sketchbooks, one finds
that certain subjects preoccupied
Marsh all his life. The hoboes lying in the sun near the railroad yards
become the derelicts he saw sleeping under the bridges of Paris, and
these are transformed into the bums
of the Bowery. Finally, all the world's
a stage, the burlesque stage. The
clown of the circus and the comedian of the burlesque are the proto-
types of all his men; the showgirl
and the striptease artist are all his
women. When Mayor La Guardia,
in an access of propriety, chased the
burlesque out of town, Marsh followed it to New Jersey. Stewart
Klonis recalls how Marsh came in to
the Art Students League, where he
was teaching a class in drawing, and
told Klonis he had just returned from
Union City and the burlesque show
there. "Since La Guardia closed them
down here, they are scared over there,
too," he said. "They won't allow
cameras; they won't even permit
sketching. But I got around that,''
and he took a tiny sketchbook, no
more than three by four inches, from
his pocket and showed it to Klonis.
"I drew *inside* my pocket," he said.
"These won't mean much to you,
but they mean something to me.''
When I think of the importance of
the burlesque to Marsh, I recall an

act I saw at the old Haymarket on
the West Side of Chicago in the early
twenties. Before a backdrop depict-
ing a city street two disreputable
characters are exchanging obscenities
when suddenly a pretty girl walks on
from the wings and minces across,
looking out at the audience, and exits
on the other side. This apparition
throws the drunken bums into great
disorder. The girl reappears and
crosses again. This time the effect is
almost disastrous. With her third
passage they are reduced to complete
helplessness. This same girl walks
down Marsh's Bowery.

William Benton says, "One of
Reg's paintings I bought largely for
the title. This is a picture of a couple
going through the Tunnel of Love at
Coney Island. The man looks pop-
eyed and scared by the terrifying
dragons and ogres. An old guard in a
gray uniform dozes. The girl, a sati-
ated blonde, looks as bored as the
guard. She looks as if she's been
through the love tunnel a bit too
often. The title of the picture when I
bought it was *The Sorrow and Futility
of Man Before the Beauty of Woman.* . . .
After a few months, Reg came to me
and wanted to borrow the picture to
send to the Carnegie Exhibit in Pittsburgh. He changed the title and
called it *Eldorado.* I told Reg that he
couldn't change the title—that I had
bought the original title. He insisted.
We never got this one settled."

If burlesque provided Marsh with
his basic form and pattern, he was
following an old and fruitful tradition. Watteau had taken the com-
media dell'arte as his pattern in
much the same way that Marsh followed burlesque, and if Watteau's
picture is elegant and gracious and
Marsh's is vulgar and tawdry, it is
the world that has changed. Artisti-
cally, Marsh was as refined as Watteau. He drew as well; his adjust-
ment of means to ends was as subtle
and perfect; his scope was greater.
John Lahr, in his biography of his
father, who had been a burlesque

comedian in his early days, has written that "the clown profanes the
world in order to define the sacred."
I believe Marsh's work tells us more
about the Decline and Fall of the
American Empire than that of any
other artist in any medium.

Only Edward Hopper was as min-
atory. I recall a big gallery of Hopper's work at the Biennale in Venice
twenty years ago. (I had the place to
myself. I believe Hopper's work is
meaningless to Europeans.) As I
went from one painting to another I
became more and more uneasy. I left
the gallery and sought fresh air outside. Then I went back to try to discover what made the work so disturbing. There was of course the
awful lower-middle-class boredom,
the lifeless edge-of-town pall, the
familiar Edward Hopper environ-
ment. But then I discovered something I hadn't noticed in Hopper's
work when I had seen his rather rare
paintings one at a time. In nearly
every picture there was a black hole,
a bottomless pit. It was the darkness
where the highway disappears into
the trees or the railroad track enters
the tunnel, and it was as if all the air
in the gallery were being sucked out
into these vents. Hopper's America is
a place of death.

I think Marsh's quality is more
profoundly unsettling than Hopper's
because Marsh was so much more
abundant. When one looks at a painting by Hopper one wonders, "Where
is everybody?" And then with Marsh
one finds, "They're all *here*!" But as
Francis Bacon observed, "Little do
men perceive what solitude is, and
how far it extendeth. For a crowd is
not company, and faces are but a gallery of pictures, and talk but a tin-
kling cymbal, where there is no love."

Marsh worked very hard and he
accomplished his mission. With the
advantage of hindsight I think I
should have realized that he was
nearly done. He said to me one day,
"I'm beginning to repeat myself."

CONTINUED ON PAGE 92

A Taste of Victory

Not so long ago, indeed well within a lifetime, there was no "dearth of heroes" in this country, to quote the title of our opening article a little out of context. At the end of what John Hay called our "splendid little war" with Spain, there seemed to be a plethora, and the occasion shown above still exudes the pride and joy of that moment. The setting is the Hudson at New York, with Grant's Tomb on the far left, and the event is the spectacular naval parade in honor of Admiral George Dewey and his thunderous victory over a Spanish fleet at Manila Bay on May 1, 1898. He lost not a man, and totally destroyed the enemy. The scene above occurred on September 29, 1899.

The little war that started out to free Cuba had ended in the acquisition of an empire in the Far East. The white man's burden had been picked up by President McKinley (following explicit instructions vouchsafed him in response to prayer, he told a conference of Methodist bishops). Now, Dewey had steamed up the harbor in his flagship *Olympia*, which appears in the foreground flying, for sentimental reasons, the burgee of that earlier hero, David Glasgow Farragut. Behind in column are *New York*, *Indiana*, *Massachusetts*, *Texas*, and an escort of cruisers and revenue cutters. The river

was awash with excursion boats, tugs, and the yachts of new millionaires. Afterward there were salutes, fireworks, electric displays, and a great parade on land led by another hero, Governor Theodore Roosevelt. No one, or almost no one, doubted the virtues of what *Harper's Weekly* proclaimed this "assertion of American power" and of "the old English temper" in our people.

In a day when world power, let alone our footholds in the Far East, seems to bring us only trouble, in times when we must tolerate the intolerable and conceive the inconceivable, and when the "old temper" has so diminished, how strange and bittersweet this triumph seems! The painting, done by the noted marine artist Fred Pansing, hangs today largely unnoticed, on permanent loan from the Museum of the City of New York, in the bar of the all-male Harvard Club of New York, whose license to serve restorative potions, we read, is threatened by an intrusive new militancy called Women's Lib. As the club's clientele changes in sex and outlook, the *Naval Parade* will no doubt wind up, like so many other things once thought proud and wonderful, in the attic.

—*Oliver Jensen*

The Radio Priest

By ROBERT S. GALLAGHER

About 1935, anno Domini, *the Reverend Charles E. Coughlin, pastor of the Shrine of the Little Flower in Royal Oak, Michigan, was perhaps the most beloved and most hated, the most respected and most feared man in the United States. His Sunday afternoon broadcasts during the thirties were avidly followed by a radio audience of between thirty and fifty million Americans, and his weekly newspaper,* Social Justice, *published by his massive National Union for Social Justice, claimed a paid circulation of well over a million. Social justice was the message he preached, and when he translated this into specific issues, thousands of Coughlinites marched at his command to the telegraph office to notify their congressmen of their leader's wishes. His denunciation of plans to have the United States join the World Court in 1935 brought 20,000 telegrams to the Senate—which rejected the plans.*

His bishop once described him as "the voice of God," and indeed, to many Americans his almost hypnotizing voice, during the confusing gloom of the Depression, seemed to proffer confidence, direction, and trust. His closest associates were charmed by his warm graciousness, his courtly manner, his infectious humor, his way with an anecdote; in a classroom, from the primary level to the university, he exhibited the rare gift of an inspired teacher.

Others—and they, too, numbered in the millions—were dismayed at the "spectacle" of a Roman Catholic priest "involved" in politics; they were suspicious of his motives and alarmed by his evident power; they read sinister implications into his utterances; they were stunned and shocked when "the radio priest" ripped off his clerical collar and denounced the President as a "liar"; they considered him, among other things, a vicious demagogue.

Coughlin backed Franklin D. Roosevelt ("It is either Roosevelt or ruin," he proclaimed) until he decided that there was nothing new about the New Deal. Convinced that the Roosevelt administration was "soft" on Communism, he launched an abortive third party in 1936, which suffered, along with Roosevelt's other opponents, ignominious defeat. In the years just prior to World War II he became increasingly isolationist and anti-Communist in his pronouncements. He was against military aid to Russia, and he opposed the entry of the United States into the war; his radio audience dwindled, and after Pearl Harbor the unabated hostility of his newspaper toward the war effort led to its

suppression by the U.S. Department of Justice. Coughlin continued as a parish priest until he retired from the Shrine in 1966.

Today, at eighty-one, he leads a quiet but active life in the comfortably sprawling, one-story home he designed and built for himself ("My third in two years," he proudly explains. "I'm a good builder. If I hadn't become a priest, I think I would have enjoyed being a carpenter"). It is in Birmingham, a few miles from the Shrine of the Little Flower, where he is listed as pastor emeritus. His daily routine is relaxed but fixed. He washes his car, attends his geraniums, and works at occasional books—theologically oriented volumes that he publishes and distributes through his own mailing list. His private chapel, in which he celebrates the Mass every morning ("I find that I say Mass now more fervently, with more devotion"), is situated between his spacious bedroom and a small study, where he displays alabaster busts of popes Leo XIII and Pius XI flanking a silver-framed photograph of his favorite bishop and personal mentor, the late Michael J. Gallagher. He no longer makes many public appearances. He avoids the press and rigorously shuns any more controversial exposure. For the past three decades he has refrained from discussing his own version of his tumultuous public career until recently he consented to talk for the historical record with AMERICAN HERITAGE.

Not many men—certainly few priests in this country—have managed such turbulent careers as yours. Looking back, can you explain this?

I was the world's greatest oddity as a clergyman—back in 1926, especially. Most Catholics at that time believed that a priest had no business in politics. He shouldn't mention anything dealing with taxation or pollution or war, you know. That's a silly notion. After all, Christ excoriated the tax gatherers and cleansed the temple of the money changers who were debasing the currency then.

And you felt that a priest had a right to get involved?

A right? The clergy had a duty to do it, not a right, a duty, even at the expense of life. You see, man is com-

Hale at eighty-one, Father Charles E. Coughlin sits for his portrait in the home he built for himself in Birmingham, Michigan.
AL KAMUDA

posed of both body and soul, and you have to take care of the total man if you're going to be a priest. Now today the tendency is to take care of the total body, and to hell with the soul. Before my time, everything was total soul. But I couldn't, I wouldn't have done what I did if I hadn't had the support of my dear friend Michael Gallagher, the bishop of Detroit. Bishop Gallagher believed as I believed, and Pope Leo XIII believed before him, and especially Pope Pius XI. Pius XI and Michael Gallagher and Joe Schrembs, he was the bishop of Cleveland, they were closest friends.

You felt, then, that you had the backing of the Church? Of the pope himself?

I believed that, even though I can't prove it today. I probably shouldn't say it, because if there was one thing I learned during my career, it is that you shouldn't say what you can't prove. But I knew, I knew what I was doing. I knew I had the authorization of the Church, because Pius XI said in 1931 that too long we have waited to intervene in these matters of taxation and carelessness over the poor and the aged and the oppressed. He was reaffirming what Leo XIII spelled out in his encyclical *Rerum Novarum*, issued in 1891, the year I was born: the Christian concept of social justice. I think Pius XI summed up this concept when he stated that it is practically impossible for a man to save his immortal soul when he is unjustly denied the goods of this world. And the first good, the most important asset, is freedom. That gift comes from God. No state can grant it, and any state that tries to deprive men of it does so at the risk of its own life. The rest—and that includes most of the social concerns that Americans are now becoming agitated about—flows naturally from this premise. So you see, everything I did and everything I said was an attempt—and I'd be the first to admit, a highly fallible attempt—to promote and exemplify the ideals of social justice spelled out by these two popes.

This is the context in which you view your work?

Yes. But there is one other thing. I am a man under authority. I believe in it, I have tried to live it, I would gladly die for it. I didn't start out that way, though. I was born in Hamilton, Ontario. My father was an American. I was the only child, and an only child, when he is a boy, is always spoiled by his mother, so they tell me. When my grandfather came to live with us, he insisted—and he had more money than he needed—that I go to a strict boarding school for my high-school education. And

it was strict. The school operated under the Holy Ghost definition of education, which was, if you recall it, teach me goodness first, discipline second, and then a poor third comes knowledge. We had the goodness preached to us and taught to us, and it was very wonderful. But the discipline was something out of this world. One night at dinner my first year, my table was headed by a philosophy senior who had been a semipro boxer. I was simply impertinent. He said something to me, and I told him to go to the devil, and he walked around and just yanked me out of my chair and floored me with one punch. That was the rule. And when I got up I had to apologize to the whole table. Frankly, it was the best thing that ever happened to me. In one instant, I learned discipline.

When you finished college you had a vocational choice between politics, sociology, and the priesthood. Is that correct?

In the professorial sense I suppose I did. I was extremely fortunate during my undergraduate years at the University of Toronto to study under several of the most brilliant teachers in the British Empire. One was James Mavor, the famous Scottish professor of political economy, who taught, among others, John Maynard Keynes. As a result I guess you could say I became a Keynesian in economics at an early age. Another was Dr. Daniel Cushing, the priest-philosopher and good friend of the Belgian prelate, Cardinal Mercier, who had helped Leo XIII write *Rerum Novarum*. I loved Dr. Cushing, and through him I came to love and revere Leo XIII.

Did these men influence you toward the priesthood?

I would say, probably. The clergy I was interested in were the Basilians, secular priests who lived in a community and were dedicated to teaching, which is what I did for six years after my ordination in 1916. When the pope disbanded these associations we were given the choice of joining a religious congregation or order, or we could remain secular priests. I chose the second option, and on February 26, 1923, I was incardinated into the diocese of Detroit by Bishop Gallagher.

You acquired an early reputation as a pulpit orator. Did this help launch your career as the "radio priest"?

No, that was purely accidental. In 1923 a close friend of mine, Dick Richards, who was the chief distributor of Pontiacs in Michigan, bought the local radio station, WJR. The studio was on the top floor of Detroit's Book-Cadillac [now Sheridan-Cadillac] Hotel, and I remember we used to have to climb an iron ladder to get into it. Well, you know radio was a pretty haphazard operation in those days. You went on the air when you could find somebody to do or say something. And occasionally I'd go over to the station and play the piano a little, or read something from Thomas Moore or Keats or Shelley or Tennyson.

Was this before you became the pastor of the Shrine of the Little Flower?

That's right. By this time I'd become the assistant secretary to the bishop, that is, his personal secretary. I handled Michael Gallagher's correspondence, not Bishop Gallagher's. Well, in 1925 he gave me the Royal Oak appointment. There was no church or anything, just a common agreement that the growth prospect of this area north of the city looked promising. He suggested I go buy some land. With what? I asked. Oh, he said, I'll cosign a note at the bank for you. That was the way parishes were established in those days. The bishop had complete confidence in his selectee. So I found a nice site out on Woodward Avenue and bought it. Then I needed about fifty thousand dollars to build a church, and I started looking around, backward instead of forward, as I should have done, and I discovered I had only twenty-eight families, thirteen of which were mixed marriages. It wasn't too bad when the husband was Catholic, but when the wife was the Catholic I couldn't expect much money. To make matters worse, soon after we started building I learned that the Ku Klux Klan was about to get a court injunction to stop the construction, something about a flaw in the deed. Well, Michigan had one of those odd laws to the effect that no injunction could be issued once the roof was on. It was the start of a three-day holiday, so I rounded up a good bunch of carpenters, and we worked around the clock, by torchlight at night, and when the court opened Tuesday morning the church was topped off, and the Klan couldn't do anything about it legally. But the money was running out, and I seemed to be losing ground every Sunday. I didn't know what to do.

So *you went on the radio?*

I went to my friends for help. There were four of us who spent a lot of time together. Dick Richards, who owned WJR, Lawrence Fisher, the general manager for many years of General Motors' Cadillac Division, and Eddie Rickenbacker. They used to call us the Evil Four.

Why?

It was just a nickname. Well, anyway, I was telling them about my troubles one night, and they suggested I try broadcasting. You go on the air, they insisted, and just tell some of the stories you're always telling us, and you'll be a big hit and get all the help you need. Well, I couldn't tell *those* stories on the air, you know. They weren't off-color stories or anything. They were the kind of stories that men tell when they're together. But they kept insisting that I try broadcasting, and that's how it started, almost accidentally.

Your first broadcast, a program for children entitled "The Golden Hour," was on October 3, 1926. The show gradually increased in popularity and was eventually carried over the Columbia Broadcasting System network. Then, on January 12, 1930, you abruptly changed the format and attacked Bolshevism. Why?

I had been doing this in the church prior to that date. I was concerned about the tendency on the part of some Democrats at that time to send aid to Russia. I didn't want the recognition of Russia until Russia recognized God. A government based on the quicksands of atheism can't be successful, because atheism saps authority. That was my contention then, and I still think I was right. You know, I don't know one people in all of history that have suffered as much as the Russians. The Irish, the Poles, the Jews, you name them. No one has ever suffered like the Russians, first under the czars, with the silent acquiescence of their bishops, and then under the Bolsheviks. Let us never forget that between 1917, when the revolution started, and 1923 about twenty-one million Russians were slaughtered, according to the estimates of our own State Department.

Why did CBS force you off the network in April, 1931?

I was stepping on the toes of money, money, money, and I was getting too close. . . . I've had a wonderful course in finance, which isn't the same as banking. I don't like talking about it, because the minute you do, you're anti this and that and the other thing, you know. At any rate, there was a tremendous amount of pressure being put on my friend Bill Paley [chairman of the board of CBS] to get rid of me. He had graciously arranged for me to go on CBS, and I owed him a debt of gratitude, and I couldn't see why he should be made to suffer because of the controversy around me. So when the network began demanding changes in my scripts, I was glad to get out. Besides, Bill taught me how to organize my own network, which I did.

Your broadcasts were soon being carried over a "network" of twenty-six independent stations from Maine to Colorado, at a cost of fourteen thousand dollars a week. Was this paid for through contributions to the Radio League of the Little Flower?

CONTINUED ON PAGE 100

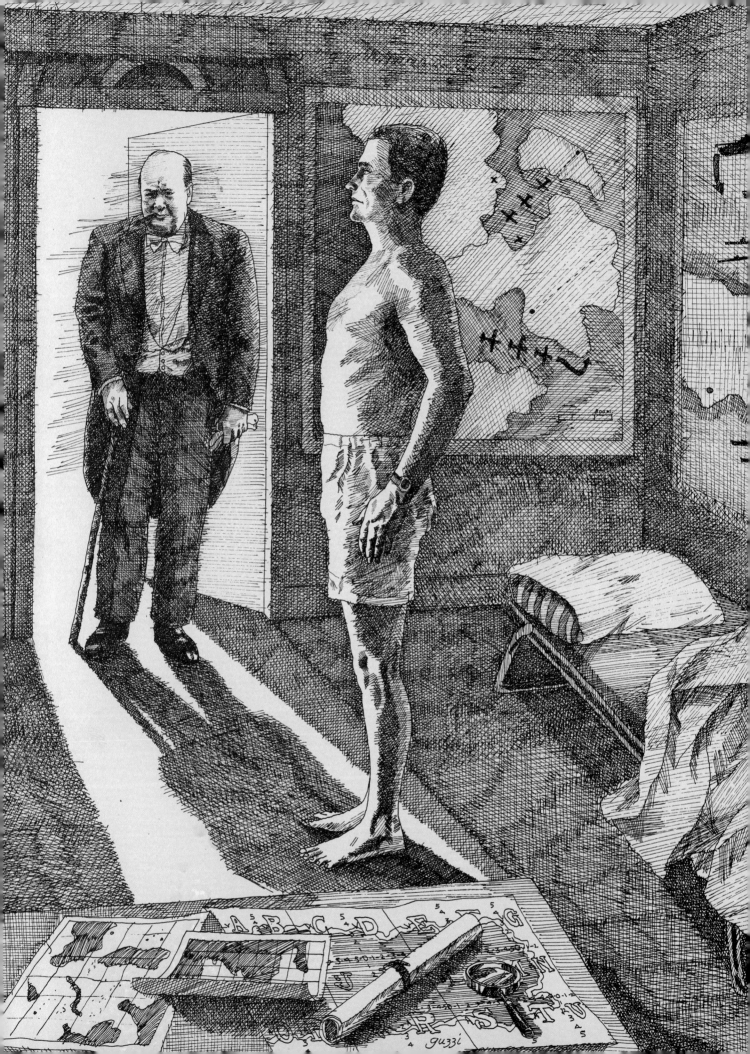

A BASEMENT VIEW OF

Sir Winston

By OGDEN KNIFFIN

At 4:30 A.M. on a cold, drizzly day in the spring of 1944, there came a knock on the guarded door of the top-secret White House Map Room. The one officer on duty opened the door to admit a rotund gentleman in white tie and tails, smoking a cigar and offering a cordial "Good morning!"

It was in a lower-floor chamber of the White House that President Roosevelt, during the war years, presided over his Map Room. Here was a repository of the highest-level information, accessible only to him and to a select group of advisers and under the command of the Presidential Naval aide. In this room Sir Winston Churchill, on many occasions, found himself at home away from home. For it was in London, directly across from Number 10 Downing Street, that he had set up what might be called the original model for F. D. R.'s Map Room. When the Prime Minister flew to Washington to consult with the President in December, 1941, he brought a portable map room with him: a collection of large-scale maps and charts showing all theatres of operation. The President observed, and shortly thereafter he directed that his own Map Room be activated.

The P.M. made many trips to Washington during World War II. There naturally was concern for his safety, and elaborate precautions were taken to conceal precise times and the mode of travel. On these visits he was always the guest of the President, rather than of the British ambassador. The reason, probably, was that here he could talk on a "feet-on-the-table" basis with the men around Roosevelt who were the decision makers—men like Admiral William D. Leahy, Harry Hopkins, and General George C. Marshall.

The daily routines of the President and of the Prime Minister differed greatly, much to the harassment of the White House domestic staff. It was the President's custom to come to the Map Room each morning about nine thirty, following a brief medical check by his personal physician. After this he ordinarily would not make use of the room again during the day, but often would return for an evening visit. The Prime Minister, on the other hand, was likely to pop in at any time, although he habitually rose later than the President and invariably tucked himself away for an hour's nap after lunch. He was a night owl by nature and often put in an appearance long after Mr. Roosevelt had gone to bed.

Between Sir Winston and Harry Hopkins, the President's confidential adviser, there was an easy rapport, a homespun air of give-and-take that I do not believe ever existed between Churchill and Roosevelt. I recall seeing the Prime Minister and Hopkins engaged in deep conversation, seated across from each other at two desks placed back to back in the Map Room. Churchill could *talk* to Hopkins, bouncing off ideas, measuring Hopkins' reaction, and contemplating how he might best present his views in a later talk with the President.

Frequently the President and the Prime Minister would arrange to meet in the Map Room for a morning conference. The P.M. invariably would get there first, moving energetically about, chatting with Hopkins, and poring over situation maps. Then would come a knock on the door, and a White House usher would say, solemnly, "The President." All would rise, those in uniform coming to attention. The President would enter in his wheelchair, assisted by a duty officer. "Good morning, Winston!" he would say; and Sir Winston would reply, "Good morning, Mr. President!" And the conference would proceed.

Churchill's pending arrival at the White House, whispered a day or two before he was due, always caused excitement in the Map Room. When the Prime Minister was aboard, as the Naval members of our group always put it, almost anything could happen.

The Map Room operated on a twenty-four-hour basis. After the change of duty at midnight, the night officer in charge had to update all situation maps as information came in, so that everything would be kept up to the minute. When things quieted down—usually about three in the morning—he was authorized to pull out a small cot and catch a few hours' sleep.

On that dank morning mentioned in the opening paragraph, I was the night duty officer. Word had been passed along that Sir Winston was to have been a dinner guest at the British embassy the previous evening. At 4:25 A.M., assuming that he must have returned and gone to bed, I pulled out the cot, stripped to my shorts, and turned in.

A few minutes later came the knock on the door and the voice of the usher: "Sir, the Prime Minister." I sprang from the cot, opened the door, and came to attention as best I could under the circumstances.

"Good evening, Mr. Prime Minister," I said. "Please come in." Sir Winston, immaculate in white tie and tails, eyed my "uniform" and said, in his gentle way, "Good morning, Captain. Perhaps it would be well for both of us to retire."

That was the last time I saw the great man.

RICHARD HOVENDEN KERN,
ARTIST, CENTRAL PARTY

CAPTAIN JOHN WILLIAMS GUNNISON,
COMMANDING, CENTRAL PARTY

DEATH STALKED

The Grand Reconnaissance

Our half-known new western empire

was mapped, in a great mass exploration, by the Army's Pacific Railroad Surveys of 1853

The reports of the Pacific Railroad Surveys are full of pictures like this one by F. W. von Egloffstein, showing the Franklin Valley in Nevada from the Humboldt Mountains, observed by a "noble savage." The Prussian artist also explored with Frémont and Joseph C. Ives.

By WILLIAM H. GOETZMANN

The Pacific Railroad Surveys of 1853 —a grand national reconnaissance extending over half a continent and led by men who would later be counted among the most prominent soldiers and scientists of the Republic —were the capstone of an American age of exploration in the Far West. They were packed with adventure and stalked by death, and they were conceived in desperation by a pre-Civil War Congress hopelessly deadlocked over the proper location for the first vital transcontinental railroad, which would link the Mississippi Valley with golden California. Should the route go north, or south? Sectionalism offered loud answers but no agreement. The railroad surveys were an attempt to let science decide a question that, after eight years of continuous debate, appeared to be beyond the powers of mortal men. Not since Napoleon, in the midst of his short-lived conquest of Egypt, had taken a large corps of savants to study that country's lands and culture had such an array of scientific talent been marshalled in the service of geographical conquest. And not since that celebrated Egyptian foray were the scientific results to prove so rich and overwhelming while the practical results appeared to lead only to frustration. For the first actual railroad to the Pacific was not completed for another sixteen years.

The great exploration provided the first panoramic view of what the vast West was really like. It produced an encyclopedia of western experience in thirteen massive calfskin volumes—government reports now consigned to dust and obscurity in public libraries and archives. In them was a matchless picture of the Old West before its settlement. The surveys likewise produced a cast of heroes—military and scientific explorers whose names and deeds, like the records of the surveys themselves, are now almost forgotten.

On the second of March, 1853,

Congress ordered the Secretary of War, Jefferson Davis, to "employ such portion of the Corps of Topographical Engineers, and such other persons as he may deem necessary, to make such explorations and surveys as he may deem advisable, to ascertain the most practicable and economical route for a railroad from the Mississippi River to the Pacific Ocean." Davis was to see to the organization and execution of the program and the compilation of a report on the findings by the first Monday in January of 1854—within ten months from the day of the order. It was a staggering assignment—one that seemed virtually impossible to complete in the time allotted, even allowing for the fact that the men were required to make only a rapid reconnaissance of the feasible routes. Moreover, with the whole project under the direction of such an arch-Southerner as Jefferson Davis some people wondered why there was to be a serious study at all, since the selection of a southern route appeared to be a foregone conclusion.

Almost immediately Davis set to work organizing the task. He established the Bureau of Explorations and Surveys, headed first by his old friend from the Topographical Corps, Major William H. Emory of Maryland, and commanded later by Captain Andrew Atkinson Humphreys, the Army hydrographic engineer who had tamed the Mississippi at the New Orleans levee. Together Davis, Emory, and Humphreys decided which routes were to be explored and who was to command each of the field parties. In general the routes considered for the surveys were those that appeared to have the most political backing in Congress. Thus, four main transcontinental parties were sent into the West, each corresponding to an important sectional interest. The northern survey, which was to operate between the forty-seventh and forty-ninth parallels, was led by Isaac Ingalls Stevens,

a brilliant and energetic young Army officer who had just resigned his commission to accept the post of governor of the new Washington Territory. This railroad route was to connect the Great Lakes to the Pacific at Puget Sound by way of St. Paul and the great bend of the Missouri River [see pages 46–47]. As the new governor, Stevens had a direct interest in bringing back a favorable report on the possibilities of the route. Moreover, his political fortunes were closely tied to those of Senator Stephen A. Douglas, chief financial backer of this northern venture.

Another expedition moved west along a line much farther south. It was led by Lieutenant Amiel Weeks Whipple, and it followed the thirty-fifth parallel from Fort Smith, Arkansas, to Santa Fe and farther westward, carrying with it the hopes of the citizens of southern Missouri, Arkansas, Tennessee, and Mississippi. Douglas also stood to profit if this line was selected, since it would connect with his new Illinois Central Railroad at Cairo, Illinois. Far to the south appeared to be the likeliest route. In fact, so convinced in its favor was Davis that at first he did not even deem it necessary to send a party out to explore it. Ultimately, however, he yielded to political pressure and ordered two expeditions into the field to survey the thirty-second parallel line—one from the west, led by the veteran explorer of New Mexico, Lieutenant John G. Parke, the other from the east, commanded by Captain John Pope, even at this early stage of his career addicted to the same self-advertisement from his "headquarters in the saddle" that would make him the laughingstock Union commander at the Civil War disaster of Second Manassas.

Out in California other expeditions coursed north and south between the Coast Ranges and the Sierras looking for passes over the mountains and for a connection between California and the Northwest.

JEFFERSON DAVIS,
SECRETARY OF WAR, 1853–57

THOMAS HART BENTON,
MISSOURI'S LONG-TIME LAWGIVER

JOHN CHARLES FRÉMONT,
EXPLORER, BENTON'S SON-IN-LAW

LT. EDWARD GRIFFIN BECKWITH
AS HE LOOKED YEARS LATER

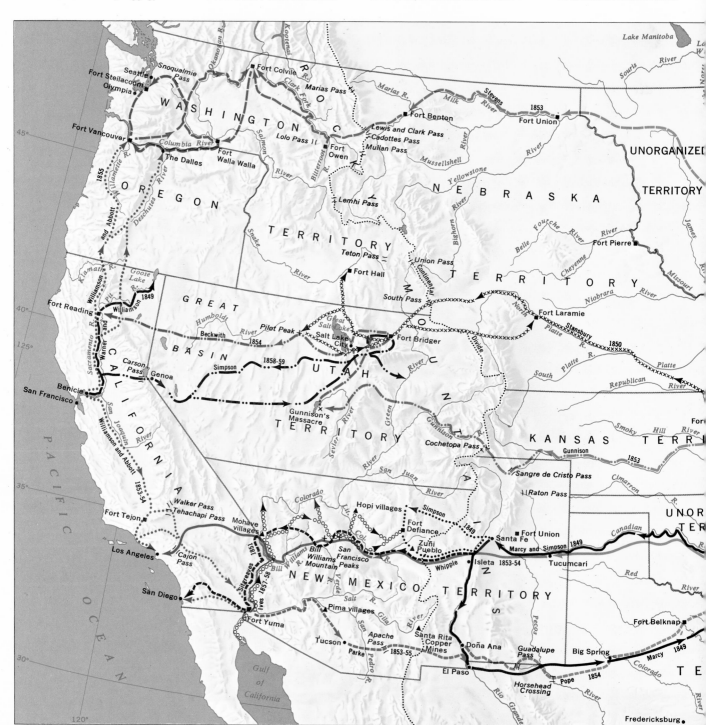

F. W. VON EGLOFFSTEIN,
ARTIST WITH BECKWITH, 1854

GOVERNMENT EXPLORATION
and SURVEYS 1849-60

←	Marcy and Simpson 1849
←•••••	Simpson 1849
← —	Warner and Williamson 1849
←xxxxx	Stansbury 1850
← — —	Sitgreaves 1851
←ooooo	Ives 1857-58
←••—••	Simpson 1858-59

PACIFIC RAILROAD SURVEYS

← —	Stevens 1853-54
←••••	Gunnison 1853
← —	Beckwith 1854
← — —	Whipple 1853-54
← — —	Pope 1854
← — —	Parke 1853-55
←•••••	Williamson and Abbott 1853-55

0   100   200   300

Perhaps the most interesting survey activity took place dead in the center of the map. Here, at the behest of the all-powerful Thomas Hart Benton, the perennial statesman from Missouri, who repeatedly called for "a grrreat central Highway to the Pacific," the Secretary sent out one of the largest and best-equipped expeditions, under Captain John Williams Gunnison of the Topographical Engineers. This expedition was to follow a line west between the thirty-eighth and thirty-ninth parallels, cross the Rocky Mountains through the Cochetopa Pass between Kansas and Utah territories, and make its way to the Great Salt Lake —which Benton and his son-in-law John Charles Frémont appear to have thought lay just due west of the celebrated Cochetopa. It was the most difficult of all the routes, and the San Juan Mountains directly in its path had been the scene of Frémont's epic disaster in 1848, when the whole party almost perished in the wintry snows and the flesh of one dead explorer was said to have been sampled by some of the starving survivors of the Pathfinder's party. Gunnison and his men seem to have believed the route to be impractical even before they started out, and the evidence indicates the possibility that Davis sent the party into the field with the object of proving Benton wrong rather than of locating a railroad route of any kind. As it was, the Gunnison survey through what is now south-central Colorado proved to be one of the most dramatic and interesting of the surveys, and thus, perhaps, it can stand here for the whole massive operation.

At the outset politics proved troublesome to Captain Gunnison. Benton, disappointed that Frémont was not picked to lead the party, thundered his defiance, and before he was through, one of Frémont's friends,

Edward Fitzgerald Beale, a hero of the war in California (he also brought the news of the gold discovery to the East), found himself made the Indian commissioner for California with a princely appropriation of $250,000 (more than the railroad survey appropriation) and orders to head west along the shortest and most practicable route. Naturally he took the great central Cochetopa Pass route, leaving in May, 1853, and arriving in Los Angeles in August. And when his friend and kinsman, newspaperman Gwin Harris Heap, finished writing a privately published report on the western march, the line through the Cochetopa Pass seemed almost incredible in its economic possibilities.

Meanwhile, back in New York Frémont himself was assembling still another force, an exploratory "truth squad," as it were, to take to the field on the heels of the Gunnison party and, presumably, challenge any unfavorable report. But Captain Gunnison was not one to be awed by such formidable competition. A tough, serious New Englander of Swedish ancestry, he was a career soldier and veteran explorer who knew the West almost as well as Frémont did. Born in 1812, Gunnison grew up on his father's farm near Goshen, New Hampshire. He attended Hopkinton Academy, taught at the age of nineteen in a one-room log schoolhouse, won an appointment to West Point in 1833, graduated second in the class of 1837, and ultimately received an appointment to the elite Corps of Topographical Engineers. As a career soldier Gunnison had an extremely varied record. He had served in Florida as an Everglades scout under Zachary Taylor. He had assisted in the sad removal of the Cherokees from Georgia to Oklahoma. He had explored and mapped parts of northern Wiscon-

This map shows the route of the Gunnison and Beckwith parties, described by Professor Goetzmann in our text; the route of the Stevens party, which we present in a separate portfolio beginning on page 49; and the remaining Pacific Railroad Surveys of 1853–55 —all in red. Other government-sponsored explorations of that era appear in black ink.

TOP FROM LEFT TO RIGHT: LIBRARY OF CONGRESS; LIBRARY OF CONGRESS; NEW YORK PUBLIC LIBRARY; U.S. MILITARY ACADEMY ARCHIVES; KANSAS STATE HISTORICAL SOCIETY, TOPEKA. MAP: FROM *The American Heritage Pictorial Atlas of U.S. History;* FOR DETAILS ABOUT OTHER EXPEDITIONS SHOWN, SEE PP. 172-73 OF THAT WORK

sin and had worked seven years on the Great Lakes Surveys learning the difficult arts of geodesy and topographical cartography. In 1849 he had ventured into the Far West as assistant to Captain Howard Stansbury in an expedition to map and explore the valley of the Great Salt Lake. There he and Stansbury spent the winter among the sometimes hostile Mormons; together, the two men got to know the ways of the West, the mountain men and hunters, the Indians, the settlers, and the mysterious Mormons themselves.

As a result of his western experience Gunnison wrote in 1852 what was perhaps the first objective book ever published about this people who so fascinated our nineteenth-century forebears: *The Mormons or Latter-Day Saints in the Valley of the Great Salt Lake.* By 1853, then, Gunnison had achieved some prominence as a soldier, author, and explorer-engineer. And though he was an outspoken advocate of a Pacific railroad, he had no sense of dedication to either St. Louis or a central route. He could be relied upon to be honest and fair in his report. In short, Gunnison was the ideal man for the job.

On June 4, 1853, one month from the date he received his orders, Gunnison had secured his scientific personnel and equipment in Washington and arrived in St. Louis for the final outfitting of his expedition. Soon he moved out onto the prairie, establishing a base camp at a one-street ramshackle trader's outpost on the Kansas River. Here he assembled his party. One of its most important members was Lieutenant Edward Griffin Beckwith, an artillery officer assigned to the Topographical Engineers who was on his second western expedition, having escorted the Collier party by way of the Gila Trail to California in 1850. Others included Frederick O. Creuzfeldt, a German botanist who had survived the disaster of Frémont's 1848 expedition; Jacob Heinrich Schiel, a geologist and Heidelberg graduate who had come all the way from Prussia to

help explore the West; Sheppard Homans, the astronomer; J. A. Snyder, assistant topographer; and Richard H. Kern, youngest of four brothers, three of whom were artists. Richard, his brother Edward, and their doctor brother Benjamin had gone along with Frémont in 1848, and Benjamin had perished somewhere in the San Juan Mountains.

By June 22 the wagons were assembled, mules broken, and equipment packed, and the Gunnison party was ready to move out—sixteen six-mule wagons, an instrument cart, and a crude canvas-topped ambulance, escorted by a contingent of thirty-two cavalrymen. They headed west along the Santa Fe Trail with the Kansas River on their right and the prairie to their left stretching away like an ocean through the rain and gloom.

Three days after the start, taking the advice of the fur-trade veterans William Bent and Tom Fitzpatrick, Gunnison divided his forces. Keeping Kern, Homans, Captain Morris of the cavalry, and a few men from the escort with him, he coursed westward along the line of the Kansas River, past Fort Riley, then only a few low adobe barracks in the process of construction, past the confluences of the Republican, Solomon, Saline, and Smoky Hill rivers with the Kansas, to an appointed rendezvous near Walnut Creek where it flowed into the great bend of the Arkansas River. Lieutenant Beckwith led the main party via the regular Santa Fe Trail until he made contact with Gunnison on the twelfth of July. At Walnut Creek they met on a great dividing line of the prairie. Behind them were the rolling swells and lush grasses of the well-watered region. Ahead lay sand and short grass, buffalo-wallow water, and prairie-dog holes, country that the earlier explorers Zebulon Pike and Stephen H. Long had called the Great American Desert.

For two weeks Gunnison pushed his party up the Arkansas, through

arid buffalo plains to Bent's Old Fort far upriver near present-day La Junta, Colorado. The fort, which William Bent had blown up himself in 1849, stood a squat and deserted adobe ruin, its rooms open to the sky, its round, castlelike tower barely discernible and fast mouldering back into the earth. It was still a landmark on the way west, but it would never again be the colorful center of frontier life it had been back in 1846, when Kearny's Army of the West camped there on the way to the conquest of Santa Fe. Beckwith, however, thought it an ideal site for a new military post at the entrance to the Southwest.

The next few days saw the explorers moving due west along the upper Arkansas, past Timpas Creek to a point on the left bank opposite Apishpa Creek, which they took to be the Huerfano River. With the utmost difficulty they managed to cross the Arkansas by sending out an advance party of several Delaware Indian scouts, who swam the river with ropes in their teeth. By August 1 the whole party had made the crossing, and far in the distance, just above the horizon, they could see the Wah-to-Yah, or Spanish Peaks, in full view.

Lacking a competent scout, they followed the Apishpa Creek southward for several days, still thinking they were on the Huerfano and that it would lead them directly to Fort Massachusetts, an Army outpost on a branch of that river in the midst of the wild and beautiful San Luis Valley. Instead the whole party became lost, and it took the services of a Spanish-New Mexican mountain man whom they ran across along the way to lead them finally into the San Luis Valley and Fort Massachusetts.

Fort Massachusetts vied with Fort Yuma as the Botany Bay of American military outposts. Situated at the base of the Sierra Blanca in the southern Rockies, it guarded the northern approaches to New Mexico, but aside from an occasional foray against the local Indians there was little else to

48

TEXT CONTINUES ON PAGE 92

ISAAC INGALLS STEVENS

JOHN MIX STANLEY

GUSTAVUS SOHON

A Picture Portfolio

The Stevens Party

Published well over a century ago, the reports of the Pacific Railroad Surveys, "made under the Direction of the Secretary of War, 1853–6," have careful maps, profile views, and illustrations of the flora and fauna and geology of the area. They also contain remarkable illustrations by the artists who went along with the various parties—but these suffer from the technical inadequacies, as far as color is concerned, of the state of printing in that era. Most of the original art itself, it was long thought, had been lost. Now, however, we have been fortunate enough to come on to a set of water colors painted for a Pacific Railroad survey, the northernmost one, made along the forty-seventh to forty-ninth parallels of latitude by Isaac Ingalls Stevens. They belong to the notable collectors Mr. and Mrs. Paul Mellon, through whose kindness they are reproduced here.

With Stevens and his subparties went two notable painters of the West, John Mix Stanley and Gustavus Sohon. The former, born in Canandaigua, New York, in 1814, was a well-known veteran of frontier travel and exploration when he joined the expedition. In 1845 he had exhibited eighty-five western scenes at a show in Cincinnati; in 1865, in the Smithsonian fire, about 146 of his paintings were destroyed. Most of the pictures here are his. Sohon, who has only two in this presentation, was born in Tilsit, Germany, in 1825, came to America at seventeen, and enlisted in the Army, becoming an acknowledged artist on the job.

Their old water colors glow and bring back to life the successful exploration of the northernmost route. Stevens, the leader, born in Andover, Massachusetts, in 1818 and graduated from West Point in 1839, had just resigned from the Army to accept appointment to the governorship of the Washington Territory. He naturally agreed to lead the survey party for a railroad that might someday bring the iron horse to his new domain at Puget Sound. The pictures by Stanley and Sohon on the pages that follow show his sure and steady progress, a much more successful passage than that enjoyed, many miles to the south, by Captain John Williams Gunnison. Stevens planned carefully and included in his plans a party heading east from the Pacific coast to meet him, under the command of Captain George B. McClellan, the future Civil War general, and a smaller supply party, led by Lieutenant Rufus Saxton, Jr. The route they travelled so arduously carries a few remaining overland trains to this day, but Governor Stevens unfortunately did not live to see them. In the Civil War, by then a major general, he fell at the Battle of Chantilly.

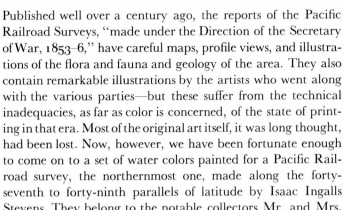

ALL ILLUSTRATIONS FROM THE COLLECTION OF

MR. AND MRS. PAUL MELLON

except as noted

TOP TO BOTTOM: NEW YORK PUBLIC LIBRARY; LIBRARY OF CONGRESS; *Smithsonian Miscellaneous Collections*, VOL. 110, NO. 7

Stevens' jumping-off place was St. Paul, Minnesota, all "vigor and activity" in 1853. The party broke camp early in June.

At Fort Union, where the Yellowstone meets the Missouri, the party paused for a week in early August. The careful Stevens met

Where the prairie gave way to high plateau, at the Sheyenne River in the Dakotas, Stanley painted the party's encampment.

the Assiniboin in council and distributed presents. Anticipating trouble, he offered every man in his party a discharge; not one accepted.

Stevens reached Fort Benton, the fur-trading post at the head of navigation on the Missouri, on September 1. He urged the Indians to keep peace among themselves.

Meat roasts on a spit while Stevens and others await the return of A. W. Tinkham, an engineer leading one of the small parties sent out on various side trips.

A dispatch has just come in from Lieutenant Cuvier Grover, sent ahead to find Lieutenant Rufus Saxton, Jr., who was heading east from the Columbia River valley with a provisioning party to meet Stevens. Stevens sits down to read it. On September 12 Saxton arrived.

OVERLEAF: *In a pine grove in the Bitter Root Valley, near the present-day Montana-Idaho border, Stevens gives a talk to a band of some fifty Nez Perces, whom he also urged to remain peaceful. He had left many troops at Fort Benton, he warned. And he offered them a council.*

The party encountered interesting sights as it headed into the Northwest, among them the Catholic mission on the Coeur d'Alene (top)—where local Indians supported themselves by farming under the guidance of the missionaries—and the abandoned Tshimakain Mission (bottom), founded by Protestants in the Spokane Indian country. By the time Stevens got there on October 24, the western party under McClellan had joined him from Fort Vancouver. Opposite is spectacular Palouse Falls in Washington.

Winter was coming on as Stevens pushed ahead. At the Bitter Root he had left behind a party under Lieutenant John Mullan, to keep contact with the Indians and explore further. Gustavus Sohon had been assigned to the party and painted its winter quarters, Cantonment Stevens, above. He also did the scene at center, opposite, of a Mullan party crossing the Hellgate River. Other groups explored the Columbia River area, including one at top, opposite, shown here by Stanley at Kettle Falls, north of where the Grand Coulee Dam was later built. The scene at bottom Stanley called Puget Sound and Mt. Rainier from Whitby Island—*the great journey's end.*

BY JOHN WESLEY JARVIS, CA. 1806; NATIONAL GALLERY OF ART, WASHINGTON, D.C.

MEN OF THE REVOLUTION — VII

The whole history of America affords examples of men who fitted precisely the needs of a particular moment, only to be cast aside, forgotten or traduced when the tide of events they created or manipulated waned and time passed them by. During and after the Revolution, it happened to James Otis and Samuel Adams, but for no one did ingratitude follow fame quite so cruelly as for Thomas Paine.

If ever a man and an idea came together at the right time, it was Tom Paine and the cause for which the colonists took up arms. When he arrived in America from England in the late fall of 1774, Paine was already a failure several times over. The son of a poor Thetford corset maker, he was apprenticed to his father, ran away to sea, jumped ship, and picked up various jobs in London—stay maker, cobbler, cabinetmaker, tax collector—never succeeding in any, edging ever closer to the cesspool of lower-class London and debtors' prison. Somehow he managed to obtain an introduction to Benjamin Franklin, who was then in England, acquired a letter of recommendation from him, and sailed from England armed with that and an abiding hatred for the rigidly structured society that had brought him to such a pass.

Through Franklin he found work as editor of the *Pennsylvania Magazine*, and thanks to an article he wrote condemning Negro slavery, he made friends with Dr. Benjamin Rush, an influential Philadelphia Whig. For an articulate, uncompromising zealot like Paine, the tense situation in the colonies in 1775 was made to order. In October he wrote an article boldly advocating separation from England and by December had completed a pamphlet on the subject that Rush, Franklin, Sam Adams, and David Rittenhouse read with uncommon interest. Rush proposed that he title it, simply, *Common Sense*.

It is worth recalling that at this point—despite the battles at Lexington, Concord, and Bunker Hill—relatively few colonists favored severing the ties with Britain. Americans generally were not thinking about independence and remained outwardly loyal to George III; their animosity was directed against Parliament and the king's ministers. What altered this state of mind so swiftly was a sudden, widespread acceptance of the ideas Paine put forth in *Common Sense*, in words that mirrored the innermost thoughts of men at every level of society in every colony. With unprecedented daring he attacked the king as a "hardened, sullen-tempered Pharaoh" and "the Royal Brute." He assailed hereditary monarchy, denounced the British establishment for exploiting the lower classes there and in America, and appealed to colonists to declare for independence and make their land a refuge for Europe's downtrodden. "Every thing that is right or reasonable pleads for separation," he argued. "The blood of the slain, the weeping voice of nature cries, *'Tis time to part.*"

Paine himself said the pamphlet sold 120,000 copies within three months; others estimated half a million; and pirated editions appeared in German, French, and Dutch. In terms of the percentage of population reached, *Common Sense* was the greatest best seller ever published in America—a booklet so exactly suited to the moment that by late spring of 1776 it had produced a wave of public feeling surging toward independence.

His next contribution came at the lowest ebb of the cause. Paine had joined George Washington's army after the defeats on Long Island and Manhattan, and he marched with the troops on their agonizing retreat through New Jersey. Having seen and borne it himself, Paine realized that there was in this extraordinary display of courage and fortitude a nobility and a source of inspiration for all Americans, could they but hear of it, and when the army arrived in Newark, he sat before a campfire and began writing, "These are the times that try men's souls: The summer soldier and the sunshine patriot will in this crisis, shrink from the service of his country; but he that stands it Now, deserves the love and thanks of man and woman." It was the first of a series of broadsides he would publish under the heading *The American Crisis*, but this one appeared when the army and the country had most desperate need of it, and the message was read to Washington's troops before their astonishing victories at Trenton and Princeton.

War's end found Paine writing a moving memorial to Congress: "Trade I do not understand. Land I have none . . . I have exiled myself from one country without making a home of another; and I cannot help sometimes asking myself, what am I better off than a refugee." New York gave him a farm in New Rochelle, but in 1787 the restless Paine went to England, where in 1791 he wrote *The Rights of Man*. In it he argued that all civil rights are based on natural rights; he advanced a farseeing concept of economic justice and social welfare, attacked critics of the French Revolution, and urged Englishmen to overthrow their monarchy. For it he was outlawed.

Fleeing to Paris, he became a French citizen, was elected a member of the Convention, and was later thrown into jail (where he completed *The Age of Reason*, a defense of deism that was unfairly condemned as an "atheist's bible"). Finally he returned to the United States, only to find that most Americans had forgotten him or had turned against him because of his radicalism or his personality (he was, a contemporary said, uncouth, coarse, "loathsome in his appearance, and a disgusting egotist").

Ignored or despised, he died in 1809. But death brought no peace to the stateless, nonconforming soul of Thomas Paine. After he was interred in a corner of his farm, vandals desecrated the tombstone before William Cobbett, the English reformer, stole his remains and shipped them to England. His bones, still unburied when Cobbett died, passed with the latter's effects into the hands of a furniture dealer to vanish forever.

—*Richard M. Ketchum*

The Observant French Lieutenant

*From
the Journal of
Comte
Jean-François-Louis
de
Clermont-Crèvecoeur*

*The Comte de Clermont-Crèvecoeur came to America in 1780 as a lieutenant in the Royal Corps of Artillery—a unit of Rochambeau's army. The young French aristocrat spent three years here and recorded them all in a journal, now translated for the first time. He proved to be an eager observer—interested in everything, open-minded, usually friendly, and tending to sweeping, youthful generalizations. As well as reporting on military matters, he described houses, people, religious customs, and food. But his principal interest was—*vive la France!—*in American women.* AMERICAN HERITAGE *presents here some brief samples of his engaging journal.*

OCTOBER, 1780

. . . The town of Newport [Rhode Island] could pass for a city, though there is nothing pretty about the town itself. Nearly all the houses are built of wood. Sometimes they build them outside the town and, when completed, put them on rollers and pull them to the lot on which they are to stand. Mostly these are very small houses, though it is not rare to see them move fairly large ones. The houses are charming, of simple architecture, and quite well planned for the convenience of each owner. The interiors are wonderfully clean, and the exteriors painted in different colors present a varied aspect that enhances one's pleasure. The Americans do not possess much furniture, barely enough for indispensable use. Everything is simple and so clean you can see your face in it.

The American manner of living is worthy of mention. Their favorite drink seems to be tea, which is ordinarily served from four to five in the afternoon. The mistress of the house does the honors. She serves it to everyone present, and it is even rude to refuse it. Generally the tea is very strong, and they put a single drop of milk in it. They also drink very weak coffee, weakening it still further with the little drop of milk. They drink chocolate in the same manner.

In the morning they breakfast on coffee, chocolate, and slices of toast with butter. They also serve cheese, jam, pickles, and sometimes fried meat. It should be remarked that those least well off always drink coffee or tea in the morning and would, I believe, sell their last shirt to procure it. The use of sugar generally marks the difference between poverty and affluence.

Their dinner consists of boiled or roast meat with vegetables cooked in water. They make their own sauce on their plates, which they usually load with everything on the table, enough to frighten a man, and pour gravy over it. On the table there is melted butter, vinegar, pepper, etc., which they use according to their taste.

In general they eat a great deal of meat and little bread, which they replace with vegetables. After dinner those in comfortable circumstances have the tablecloth removed, whereupon the ladies retire. Madeira wine is brought, and the men drink and smoke for quite a while. Among the prosperous, and especially at dinner parties, after the ladies retire the customary healths are drunk; there are so many that one rarely leaves the table without being a little tipsy from the vapors of the wine and the noise the men make when the wine begins to go to their heads.

At meals a bowl containing grog, cider, or beer is passed to those who are thirsty. (Grog is a drink made of rum and water; when there is sugar in it, it is called toddy, and if lemon is added, punch.) There are no glasses, but always this inevitable bowl that is presented to you. When you go visiting, the master of the house never fails to offer you a drink. He takes one first, being careful to drink to your health. Then comes your turn. . . .

The Americans are tall and well built, but most of them look as though they had grown while convalescing from an illness. (There are some, however, who are big and fat, but not very vigorous.) The Americans do not live long; generally one notices that they live to be sixty or seventy, and the latter are rare. There are, however, men and women here of eighty, but it is exceedingly uncommon for them to reach that age. I knew one man who was ninety and still rode horseback with ease, was possessed of all his faculties, and enjoyed perfect health.

The women are also very pale and seem frail. They are quite precocious. A girl of twenty here would pass for thirty in France. It must be admitted, though, that nowhere have I seen a more beautiful strain. As I have said, the women have very little color, but nothing can compare with the whiteness and texture of their skin. They have charming figures, and in general one can say they are all pretty, even beautiful, in the regularity of their features and in what one can imagine to be a woman's loveliest attribute.

One must see them at a dance, where they acquire the color they do not have naturally; then one is really struck with admiration. But they are displeasing in one very noticeable respect, and that is their cold manner. Once off the floor, they lose much of their charm and show little vivacity and gaiety in your company. If you do not want to be bored, you must assume the burden of conversation, animating it with our French gaiety, or else you will be lost. It is very difficult to make such an effort, especially when you do not know English. However, when these beauties get to know us, and when they deign to let us look at them, we find them absolutely ravishing. . . .

. . . Few members of the army had cause to complain of their lodging or their hosts. Nevertheless, one may reasonably state that the character of this nation is little adapted to society. The men are very cold, rather stiff, and reticent, except for a group called Quakers. . . .

[The Quakers'] form of worshipping the Supreme Being seems rather bizarre. Their meetinghouse is open to all. They assemble there twice on Sunday, morning and evening. The sexes are separated, and one never sees men sitting in the women's pews. The utmost silence reigns, and the members of the sect seem lost in the deepest reflection. Everyone is seated. When they feel so inspired, the men, as well as the women and girls, may speak. Whoever finds himself in this condition is easy to detect by his convulsive movements: his voice, his body, and all his limbs become agitated. Then everyone awaits the gift of the Holy Spirit and prepares to listen to the discourse that follows these quakings. It often happens that they leave the meetinghouse without having uttered a word. . . .

This sect is very rigid, as I have said above. Quakers allow themselves no pleasures beyond conversation and meditation; they are forbidden to sing and dance. The women, who are very pretty and are more inclined to pleasure than those of other sects (and that is not surprising, considering the constraint under which they must live), cannot become accustomed to such rigorous behavior, particularly while they are young and pretty. They detest their religion and only come to like it at an age when French women begin to become devout. If the Quaker men are even more solemn than those of other sects, one finds that Quaker girls balance the score by being much gayer and more playful. They love pleasure but are always held back by the fear of displeasing their parents. Since they have no ministers, they have no ceremonies. They marry themselves in the presence of all their friends and relatives, promising mutual fidelity. They publish banns and sign a contract in order to ensure that their mutual possessions benefit their children. Their wedding feasts are terribly dreary, since nobody speaks. You may imagine how much fun that must be! . . .

AUGUST, 1781

. . . This . . . leads me to make a brief observation on the subject of American women, or girls. In a country so new, where vice should not be deeply rooted, why should there be such a large number of prostitutes? Only one reason seems to me to be the cause. Although the fathers and mothers keep an eye on their daughters during their childhood, once they reach the age when human nature demands that they know everything, they become their own mistresses and are free to keep company with anyone they wish. Among the country people (for today in the towns education has corrected the abuses of which I shall speak) the girls enjoy so much freedom that a Frenchman or an Englishman, unaccustomed to such a situation, straightaway seeks the final favors. It is actually the custom, when a young man declares himself to be in love with a young girl, without even mentioning marriage, to permit him to bundle with her. This permission is granted by the parents. He then shuts himself up in a room with the young lady to lavish the most tender caresses upon her, stopping short of those reserved for marriage alone; otherwise he would transgress the established laws of bundling. If the young lady should take offense at his intrepidity, her parents will give him a hard time. The truly virtuous girls, who are not governed by temperament, easily resist and conform to the letter of the law of bundling, but it is to be feared that those more amply endowed by nature in this respect succumb to this tender sport. Bundling, it would seem, is made for Americans only. The coldness and gravity of their faces proclaim that this sport suits them perfectly. The bundling period is not defined; you can play this game for five or six years before deciding to marry, and even afterwards if you wish, without committing yourself finally to marry the girl after receiving these initial favors.

The women are generally very faithful to their husbands. You find few libertines among them. Yet some girls lead a most licentious life before they marry, though once married they, too, become good. The men are not fussy in this respect; they believe a girl should be free and do not despise her unless she is unfaithful after marriage. Thus a girl who has proved her worth, if she is pretty or rich, is quite sure of finding a husband; if she has had the misfortune to be seduced and the seduction bears its unfortunate fruit, it is not she who is disgraced, but the man. Respectable houses are henceforth closed to him, and he cannot marry into a respectable family.

It is rare to find a woman committing adultery here, though it does happen. In this situation the husband announces the delinquency of his wife and publishes it in the papers. No dishonor falls upon the husbands for the misconduct of their wives, and no one points the finger of scorn at a cuckold. Instead, they pity him. If the wife absconds with her lover, the husband announces in the gazette that his wife has quit his bed and declares that he will not pay her bills or be liable for any debts she may have contracted. The husband always assumes responsibility for his wife's obligations, but in this circumstance his conscience is clear, since a wife who abandons her husband becomes a criminal. This is no excuse, however, for dissolving the marriage, which rarely occurs, since their laws do not permit it. The husbands are quite patient about waiting for their wives to repent. If they do, their husbands take them back, forget the past, and live with them in perfect harmony. I leave it to the European husbands to ask themselves whether they are capable of doing as much. . . .

Clermont-Crèvecoeur's journal, from which this excerpt is taken, is one of the documents which will be included in The American Campaigns of Rochambeau's Army, 1780–1783, *edited and translated by Howard C. Rice, Jr., and Anne S. K. Brown. This two-volume work will be copublished in November by Princeton University Press and Brown University Press. The journal itself is the property of The Rhode Island Historical Society.*

THE NATIONAL POLICE GAZETTE

THE LEADING ILLUSTRATED SPORTING JOURNAL IN AMERICA.

Copyrighted for 1890 by the Proprietor, Richard K. Fox, Franklin Square Publishing, Printing and Engraving House, New York City.

RICHARD K. FOX,
Editor and Proprietor.

NEW YORK, SATURDAY, SEPTEMBER 27, 1890.

VOLUME LVII.—No. 681.
Price Ten Cents.

THE GIRLS BIFFED EACH OTHER.
MAMIE HERBETT AND MABEL BROWN FIGHT FOR GEORGE WOODWARD IN PLEASANTVILLE.

No one, it has been said, ever really learns to accept the fact that it was a coupling by his parents that produced him. The novelist Louis Auchincloss extends this and says we can never believe in the sexuality of our grandparents.

When we go back even beyond our grandparents and their contemporaries, questions of procreation become unimportant when compared to the struggle that must be made to believe that these people actually existed. I myself fought this battle for the ten years that I gave to the writing of three books. Sitting in the Manuscripts Division of the Library of Congress, fingering letters forgotten these fifty years, I would think, "How marvelous and touching"; and standing on hillocks in Flanders surrounded by the graves of the New Army of 1916's Great Britain, I found it hard not to weep—but I always had the very strong feeling that I was not dealing with anything real. The past, yes. Characters in history. Dust. But not real people.

I would argue with myself, saying, "Look, these people from history—all these people from history, Saladin, the Boys in Blue at Gettysburg, the brokers on Black Thursday in 1929 —they must have felt cold in the February of their years, must have felt the need of rest rooms upon occasion. They couldn't have run around being historic *all* the time."

But in my deepest self I would think, "No, not they. They would have been too entranced with the fascinating times in which they lived to bother about trifles. I can't think of Runnymede or the Kaiser's headquarters in 1918 or the Pope and Charlemagne on Christmas Day of 800 and think at the same time of business worries or hunger or desire for a warm bed."

Now, we all have pictures of various periods of history, pictures in our minds that are thrown on our mental projection-screens by words. Consider, for example, a brief period in a specific place: the 1880's and 90's in America. We think of the hotels of Metropolis filled with new-made rail millionaires wolfing it down at the oyster bar; we think of hansoms, sulkies, Conestogas, and summertime awnings and shaved ice with syrup, and lads wearing overalls with suspenders, and the schoolmarm in leg-of-mutton sleeves passing along the wooden sidewalk, past the drummers making a spittoon ping. Those times in that place mean sweatshops and horse wagons bringing the milk to the early train, outdoor privies, child labor, bandstands and trolleys and the jamborees of the Grand Army of the Republic.

Are you really able to believe all this and place yourself there, sitting on the porch with a schooner of beer after your long trudge home from the mill? I doubt you can. It was something people write about, but it wasn't real. It was Edith Wharton and Booth Tarkington and a whole host of movies with "Casey would waltz with the strawberry blonde"

being sung in the background; it was dreams and novels and Sister Carrie and The Good Old Days. But not reality. Can you really smell coal dust and feel the pull of muddy streets on your boots, can you believe in one suit for go-to-church, and work clothes all the rest of the time? Can you feel all that and believe in it? I doubt you can.

I never could—and still cannot. But I'm closer now to what it all must have been like. I've read the *Police Gazette*.

The *Police Gazette* began publication in 1845 with the idea of writing about highwaymen and suchlike malefactors, the thought being that the public would get on to the evildoers and fix their wagons. The magazine was a kind of early-day *True Detective Stories*. Only a couple of years after publication began, the country went to war with Mexico. The United States War Department, plagued by desertions, then subsidized the paper so that it would reveal on its back page each week the information that So-and-so, five feet four, scar on right hand, civilian occupation cooper, had gone AWOL from the 8th Dragoons. When the war was over, the paper went back to endless descriptions of the doings of civilian criminals. The chaps in the dreary stories bereft of the slightest tinge of literary panache still seemed to have a command of English that the most meticulous old-maid schoolteacher would envy: "Stand and deliver, lest I upon the moment discharge the contents of this blunderbuss forthwith."

For thirty years the *Police Gazette* drifted downward. Sometimes it roused itself for an exposé of some particular outrage, and there might be a lively reaction, with bands of criminals stoning the paper's building in lower New York. But for the

The dapper publisher of the lurid Police Gazette: *Richard Kyle Fox, in his heyday*

MLLE. D'ARY.
ONE OF THE MOST SHAPELY ACTRESSES OF PARIS IN A
NEW AND VERY CHARMING POSE.

COLLEGE GIRLS FIGHT FIRE.

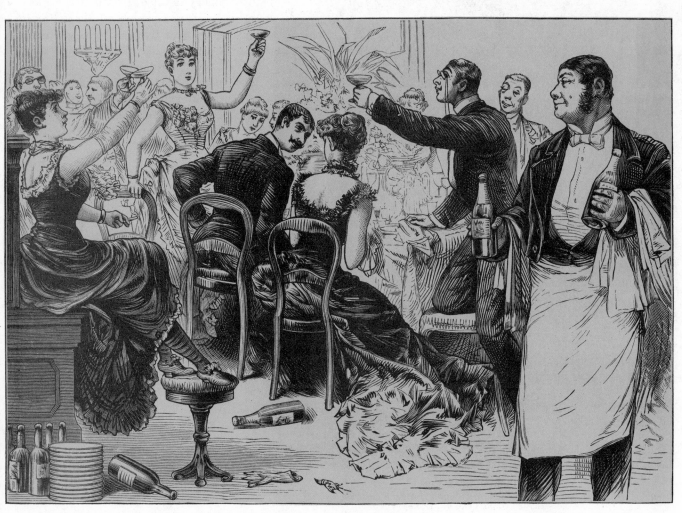

DUDES AND BURLESQUERS.
THE JOLLY MIDNIGHT RACKET TENDERED LONDON "GAIETY" CHORUS GIRLS BY "TONY" NEW YORK MASHERS.

most part it was heavy and dull. On the side it sold immunity to *real* crooks, taking hush money whenever offered. It was the oldest weekly in the country, but it was a bore.

Enter Richard Kyle Fox. He was from Belfast, the grandson of a minister. He came to America in 1874, and, according to the story he later told, he got into a brawl on the very pier that had felt his first footsteps in the New World only moments before. One of his fellow punchers turned out to be an employee of the *Commercial Bulletin*, which was the *Wall Street Journal* of its day. The man, a Mr. O'Brien, took Fox around to his office and got him a job as an advertising salesman. Fox was a whiz at that. On the side he sold ads for the doddering *Police Gazette*, which was then owned by two engravers, a father and son who had taken it over in payment for debts owed them by the previous management. Within two years their own obligations to Fox led them to unload their half-moribund rag on him as a settlement.

Fox's character was such that the words "good taste" can be applied to him with as much reason as "nice fellow" to Genghis Khan. Vulgarity was his middle name. "Wooly-Headed African Half-Ape Stretched From Tree By Righteous Mississippi Gentlemen" ran the headline on a story typical of those with which he filled his new acquisition. "Sheeny Abortionist Trapped By Brave Beauty." Fox was a good hater. He disliked clergymen, all foreigners, the upper classes of society, politicians. He was not fond of college boys or doctors. In addition he was abominably devoted to self-glorification. No member of his writing staff ever got a real by-line—some got noms de plume like "Paul Prowler" or "The Old Rounder"—but Fox's own name often appeared, and usually in capital letters. Frequent tribute was paid to his grit, mental acuteness, dauntless courage, generosity, and indomitable will.

Fox, then, was bigoted, narrow, shameless, and more than slightly ridiculous. He was also a genius.

For he invented the sports page and the gossip column, and he was the first to use copious illustrations to dramatize the stories in his paper. Before Fox, these things really did not exist. Because of him prize fighters were suddenly fascinating public figures, and so were actresses and chorus girls. And wonderful, dramatic woodcuts made something of little people in towns no one had ever heard of, showed them doing things, told something about them.

Anything Fox ever said about himself in print has to be discounted by at least half, so it is difficult at this late date to discuss just how his

WHO MURDERED EMMA?
MISS PFITZENMYER, A GERMAN MADCHEN, HAS A GOOD TIME AT A CHESTER, PA., BALL AND IS THEN FOUND DEAD IN HER ROOM.

paper was written each week. He would have it that a vast corps of *Police Gazette* reporters snooped around the entire continent, keeping their eyes open for news. In reality the paper seems to have relied a great deal upon regular daily newspapers whose stories could be rewritten to *Police Gazette* standards. (For very important, continuing stories, Fox did send his own men out.)

When the various stories, however obtained, were selected by Fox himself for airing in his pages, he would have his writers locked into a large room. Most of his writers were not full-time employees but reporters for New York's more than a dozen daily newspapers, who, attired in capes and living in furnished rooms two blocks from their offices, subsisted on drink and the dream of a big scoop. In their big room at the *Police Gazette* they would be given all they wanted to drink and also good food. Plug-uglies—boxers and wrestlers who hung around Fox—lounged outside the door. This was all done on weekends, when the reporters were free from their regular jobs. On Monday morning, if the assigned work had been satisfactorily completed, the writers would be let out into the air and pointed in the direction of their regular offices. Each man bore away a ten-dollar bill.

It is certain that some of these anonymous scribes were major-leaguers, and in fact legend has it that all kinds of great talents labored for the booze, eats, and tenner. The brevity and sharpness that characterize some of the stories of prostitutes taking their own lives, of men going up to the scaffold, of life and death a long time ago, indicate abilities of a higher order than a hack possesses. Upon occasion the human sympathies of a writer come through despite the smart-aleck quality of much of the paper's content. It is also worth saying that almost alone of America's press the *Police Gazette* saw in the actions of Henry Clay

COOKED ON A RED HOT STOVE.
FRANK CODY, A NEW MEXICO RANCHMAN, SHOT ALMOST TO DEATH AND THEN ROASTED ALIVE BY INDIANS.

Frick at Homestead the attitude of a damnable murderer. And while Fox's demonic hatred of Orientals is held directly responsible for the Chinese Exclusion Acts and an American attitude toward Asians that is still bringing tragic results, he did a good deal toward pointing out the horrors of transatlantic steerage conditions. To his credit it also can be said that he gave Victorian cant its comeuppance—in spades. I would say that this short list, to which we will add his race prejudices, exhausts those items upon which we can pass moral judgment, favorable or otherwise. For the *Police Gazette* did not exist for the discussion of great issues. It stood for entertainment, raciness, and readability.

As for pictures, the *Police Gazette* was supreme. Its woodcuts have never been surpassed. Their technical detail in the period before the photograph came in with a rush was a wonder of journalism. The artists, full-time employees, worked usually from imagination, occasionally from direct observation. The details of the clothing portrayed, the wagons, buildings, kitchens, implements, and the old-fashioned faces, give us as good a picture of those days as is likely to be found.

The heart and soul of the *Police Gazette* consisted of sports and theatre coverage, plus crime and Sin. Fox, by creating wild definitions, managed to include almost every phase of human activity imaginable under

AT THE STUDENTS' BALL.

HOW A NEW YORK SPORT AND A NEW ENGLAND SERMON SLINGER WERE INTRODUCED
TO THE CAN CAN AND THOSE WHO DANCE IT, AND WHAT FOLLOWED, IS TOLD
IN FULL IN "PARIS INSIDE OUT."

tough Boston lad who was pointed out as a comer in the prize ring—in which disputes were settled by 100- or 115-round bare-fisted contests. Fox told a waiter to have the fighter come to his table. In reply to the waiter's request, the tough said, "It's no farther from him to me than it is from me to him. If he wants to see John L. Sullivan, he can do the walking."

This to the proprietor of the *Police Gazette!* Fox set out to destroy the thug. He imported English brawlers and New Zealand sluggers; he brought forth Hibernian bravoes and American heroes and charged them one by one to humble John L. They all failed, but the prefight build-ups—Ryan and Wilson and Mitchell and Greenfield and Slade sawing wood, doing roadwork, eating raw steak, pitching hay—set sporting America aflame.

Eventually Fox came up with Jake Kilrain, whom he presented in his paper as a knightlike figure who talked in gravely polite tones and never ventured into the street without his high silk hat. For various reasons, Sullivan did not immediately arrange to battle Kilrain. Booming that Sullivan feared his man, Fox anointed Kilrain as America's champion and sent him to England to take on Jem Smith, the British titleholder. The two slugged at each other for hours, until darkness made it impossible for them to go on. Fox decided that although officially the bout was a draw, Kilrain was the winner and hence, by his logic, the champion of the entire world.

The decision was more or less accepted by sporting gentlemen everywhere, even as they accepted the *Police Gazette*'s highly popular column of answers to sports questions as the final determiner of all bets. But there remained Sullivan. When John L. agreed to meet Kilrain, the whole country held its breath waiting for the outcome. To the chagrin of the *Police Gazette,* Sullivan won. After

the category of sports. He sponsored bizarre contests for which he offered Championship Belts adorned with his name and that of his publication. Without his inspiration it is doubtful that America would have had a Champion Hog Butcher, Water Drinker, and Teeth Weight Lifter.

More significant were his contributions to boxing. Had Fox never lived, Dempsey and Louis and Ali might have lived out their years fighting on barges moored in rivers where the sheriff ventured not. Al-

most alone, the *Police Gazette* made boxing big business and so popular that the result of a Sullivan-Ryan bout was of immensely more interest to the citizens than the result of a Garfield-Hancock Presidential election.

Fox was interested in all classes of fighters and faithfully gave his Championship Belts to men of all weight divisions. But his passion was for the heavyweights. In 1881, at the Gentlemen's Sporting Theatre in New York's Bowery, he saw a brutally

that there was nothing to do but make it up with the Boston Strong Boy. He was given the Championship Belt and is remembered as the first of the official heavyweight champions.

Fox campaigned to make boxing not only popular but legal. (Both the Kilrain-Jem Smith and Kilrain-Sullivan bouts violated the laws of the places where they were held.) He ended by making the sport respectable. In the ten years that elapsed between the moment of Sullivan's insulting remark in the Gentlemen's Sporting Theatre in New York and Sullivan's defeat by Jim Corbett in New Orleans, boxing came of age. Before and after this happy ending, Fox continued wildly to push all sports: rat killing, lady wrestling, one-legged clog dancing, water walking, everything. He himself knew very little about the technical details, but it did not matter. Our great-grandparents lived lives that generally precluded visiting a big city more than once or twice in a lifetime. They had no television, no movies, no radio. Where the European peasantry to a certain extent partook of the great world through their interest in His Royal Highness or Her Imperial Majesty, Americans lived in part through their interest in sports heroes whom they would never see in the flesh. Fox understood that. There was not a saloon or barbershop, not a club or volunteers' firehouse that in time did not hang in a prominent place a portrait of John L., or Corbett, or, later, Bob Fitzsimmons. Those pictures were purchased from the *Police Gazette* printing plant in the giant building at Franklin Square, New York City—the country's largest newspaper building, Fox often pointed out—and it was Richard Fox who created the interest that made men hang those pictures up on the wall.

In the America where the *Police Gazette* flourished, every town, even the smallest, had a Bijou Theatre or a Gayety. (In my own small town in upstate New York, the space above what is now our local drugstore was, from 1880 to 1900, referred to as the Grand Opera House.)

The lighting was terrible in these places, and the stage boards creaked. But down the street was a depot—in my town there were, in fact, three depots, and now, of course, there are none—and from time to time there arrived a troupe of touring players. Out in the dreary prairie hamlets the players got off the cars covered with dust; in the South they would be sweaty all over. Their costumes were frayed. Nevertheless, they represented glamour equally mixed with Sin. The very words used for the feminine players were charged with excitement for the mill hands and cowmen: *soubrette, ballet girl.*

The dramatic plays were old reliables in which the villain got his in the last act. The musicals were loud. The comedians were far from the polished performers of the vaudeville days of thirty years later. But these troupers brought the great world to the little lonely towns on the great continent that in the late nineteenth century was essentially unpeopled and undeveloped. The players brought a bit of color with them and left behind inflamed farm boys and, sometimes, farm girls who, though forbidden to go to the performance, might have caught enough of a glimpse of the players in the street to engender the hope that they, too, might someday drink champagne—"wine," it was called—and have a handsome leading man and go about in a flare of glamour—and be something. Be an actress.

The clergymen thundered against all this. (A story has come down over the years that a group of reverends called upon Fox in his office, bearing, with horror, a picture he had published of a vilely exposed soubrette. "Let us pray!" cried the leader of the dominies, and Fox at once dropped to his knees before his desk and chanted away for a while. After that there seemed nothing for the men of God to do but take their leave.) Constables threatened action if performances should prove obscene, and good ladies flounced away when the sinners appeared on the streets near their hotel. But the thea-

EFFECTS OF THE BROOKLYN CHURCH REVIVAL.
REFERENCE TO THE SCANDAL CAUSES THE GUSHING PASTOR, BEECHER, TO WEEP—HIS LADY MEMBERS COME TO THE RESCUE AND SOOTHE THE OLD DOMINIE IN HIS TEARFUL TROUBLE.

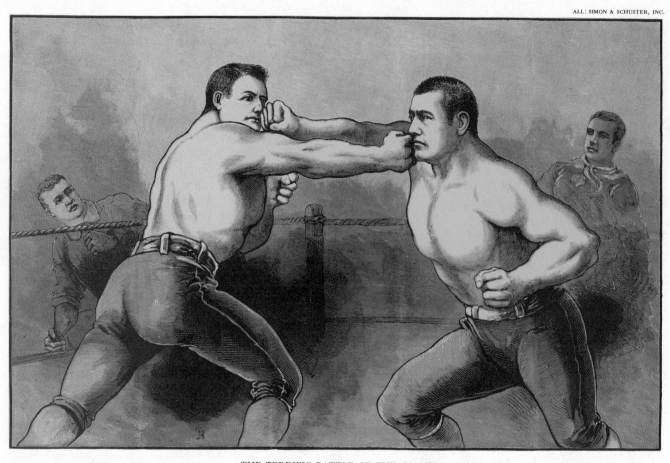

THE TERRIFIC BATTLE OF THE GIANTS.
JAKE KILRAIN AND JOHN L. SULLIVAN FIGHTING FOR THE $20,000 STAKES,
THE "POLICE GAZETTE" CHAMPION BELT AND THE CHAMPIONSHIP OF THE WORLD, AT RICHBURG, MISS., JULY 8, 1889.

tre flourished in those years.

It might not have done so handsomely had the *Police Gazette* never been. Before Fox, the stage people had gone almost wholly unchronicled. Fox saw them as aids to circulation, and to this end not an issue of his paper appeared without some theatre gossip, some discussion of players' love affairs and plans, and—most important of all—at least one Favorite of the Footlights to set the pulse beating. To our eyes these girls seem unbelievable—incredibly thick of limb, heavy of jowl, arch of countenance, cow-eyed—but to our great-grandfathers they were spicy, daring, exciting, stimulating, all that Theatre was supposed to be.

Our great-grandparents for the most part lived their lives on the scanty proceeds of damned hard work and damned long hours in foundries and blacksmith shops, in sawmills and factories and sweatshops and farm fields, in tobacco-stripping plants and lumberyards, in kitchens sweltering in summer and freezing in winter—but a very tiny percentage of them lived in the Gilded Age. For these few, the actress was as much a part of education as Princeton or Harvard. The dudes and swells had to have their fling. And the girls at Vassar naughtily experimented with cigarettes and the wearing of trousers. These scandals were always grist for Fox's mill. Sin —that sold papers. And how Fox ranted against it!

But, of course, the *Police Gazette* itself was sinful. When you get right down to it, that is what it was. The illustrations showed women's *ankles*. All the time! In every issue! Writing in 1930, the renowned columnist Franklin P. Adams, looking back to his youth, said that the pugilistic stuff never had interested him— what got to him was the ankles. "Yes, I used to stare at those pictures, and so did all the boys that I knew."

Fox never came out and said that ankles and even knees were the subjects of half the illustrations. It was just that women tended to fight with one another in Kenosha, or get tossed by a steer in Laredo, or get caught in barbed wire in Rochester —and when this happened, their skirts jumped up. And sports reading of these events and studying the woodcuts in an atmosphere of cigars and bay rum—for the true home of the *Police Gazette* was the barbershop and saloon—well, they read and studied. Who can blame them? They lived in towns in which the street paving ended where the trolley made its turnaround. Their wrists were thick and their nails dirty. They drank, being largely of the lower orders (as was 95 per cent of the population) and therefore pretty much immune to the genteel Women's Christian Temperance Union ideas of the middle classes. Their surroundings were grimy and dreary: coal dust in the winter and mud in the spring and the smell of horse manure all year round. There was precious little spice in their lives. So they looked at ankles.

But, you know, they were our own. History, as History, was not for them or for their *Police Gazette*. There was never the slightest mention of History in the pink pages upon which the paper was printed. (Why pink pages? Nobody knows for sure. It was a Fox inspiration, and it worked, it caught the eye and imagination.) History was our immigration policy, or foreign affairs, or the tariff issue. It was the little printed phrases in the left-hand corners of school textbooks—The Currency Issue, The Interstate Commerce Act of 1887, Federal Grants to Western States. None of that will you find here in what used to be called "The Pinky." The readers might have guffawed at "Prominent Banker Pushes Peanut With Nose For a Mile to Pay Off Election Bet," but if they wanted to know about Grover Cleveland's policies, they would have to seek elsewhere. That must have been the way they wanted it. Otherwise the paper wouldn't have sold.

Great-grandmother and great-grandfather have now gone to dust under cemetery stones. We have pictures of them in old albums, and in those pictures he is sitting sternly, wearing, always, a coat and tie. She is straight-backed and staring at the camera with her hand placed on his shoulder. She buried half her brood because the sickness carried them off, and he slaved like a dog in the fields or along the railroad line, but you would never know it from the prim

picture taken by a studio photographer, telling them not to move for the long period it would take for an exposure to be made. But beyond those unsmiling faces and his whiskers and her hairdo and long skirt you can sense, if you take the *Police Gazette* for what it was, that these stern, heroic figures were, after all, real. Like us. Their country lanes are superhighways now, and so much of it all is gone—kerosene lamps, the stoves, sleds, saws for cutting the ice, stickpins, and needle workshops . . . everything. But something of it all is in the pages of the *Police Gazette* to say that once upon a time these our own breathed, yelled, fought, made love, had great and terrible passions, laughed—that they lived.

Richard Kyle Fox died in 1922, a multimillionaire. By then his paper had been in decline for twenty years. Hearst and Pulitzer and McCormick long afterward admitted their debt to him, saying that the New York *Daily News* and Chicago *Tribune* were his heirs. Their time began when his ended. He had less than twenty-five years for his run. Then, around the turn of the century, the dailies, copying him, outsensationalized and out-yellow-journalized him. On top of which, they had photographs, too.

Fox, no longer young, tried to hang on through the days just before and after the First World War. But the life and the spirit weren't there any more. The dailies had sports sections and theatrical columns, too. By the time he died, his paper was as dull and lifeless as it had been when he began.

Ten years after his death the *Police Gazette*, trapped by the Great Depression, was sold for a bankrupt. A few years later, Harold Roswell took it over. He breathed some life into it, bringing it out as a monthly. Then a Canadian outfit bought it. You see it on your newsstand, sometimes. I do not believe it will come back big again.

This article is taken from the introduction to The Police Gazette, *an anthology of articles from that journal that Gene and Jayne Barry Smith have compiled for Simon & Schuster. It will be published next month.*

STEVE BRODIE'S MIRACULOUS FEAT.
THE POLICE GAZETTE AERIAL JUMPER DROPS OVER TWO HUNDRED FEET FROM THE POUGHKEEPSIE BRIDGE, PUTTING ALL PREVIOUS BRIDGE JUMPS IN THE SHADE.

JAGUARINA.
READY AND WILLING TO MEET ANY SWORDSMAN IN THE WORLD MOUNTED OR AFOOT.

LINCOLN SAVES A REFORMER

The Navy and contractor Smith accused each other of fraud.
The Navy won—until the President took a hand

The way of the reformer is hard. The way of that idealistic David who slings his polished stones at the Goliath of military bureaucracy is trebly hard. He needs a firm heart and strong friends. Franklin W. Smith, the principal in a celebrated naval court-martial during the Civil War, found one such just and farseeing advocate in Abraham Lincoln.

Without the President's help Smith would have lost everything—business, fortune, reputation, health, freedom itself. Even with Lincoln's last-moment intervention, he went through a prolonged agony that would have utterly overwhelmed a less dedicated idealist. It is disquieting to note, too, that if Lincoln had not acted when he did, Smith's unjust sentence might have been executed. For this was probably Lincoln's last act of personal justice; he was assassinated less than four weeks later.

Smith's difficulties began on the morning of Bunker Hill Day, June 17, 1864. Across the harbor Charlestown was noisily celebrating the famous battle for freedom, but Boston was quiet. The stores were closed. Through the half-deserted streets marched squads of the 13th Veteran Reserves. With no warning and no warrant except a telegraphed order from the Secretary of the Navy, they seized Smith, a prominent young merchant and Sunday-school superintendent. Giving him no chance to see his ailing wife or even to put on adequate clothing, they dragged him to a waiting tug and carried him across the harbor, chill in a blustery east wind, to Fort Warren on bleak Georges Island.

Meanwhile other soldiers and marines were battering through the door of his hardware store, ransacking his office, and, with the help of a locksmith, forcing his safe. Shortly afterward, still with no warrant, they roughly invaded his home on Shawmut Avenue. They searched it thoroughly, even breaking open the locked drawers in the desk in his bedroom and confiscating his own and his wife's most intimate family letters. This rude invasion, intensely embarrassing to Mrs. Smith, who was pregnant, was the first notice she or Smith's aged parents had of his arrest. In the afternoon of the same day, Franklin Smith's older brother and partner, Benjamin, was arrested in similar manner at his home in Cambridge. At Fort Warren, where both were lodged, only the humanity of the commandant, who invited them to his own lodgings, kept these men of high reputation from being herded in with Rebel prisoners and hardened malefactors.

The following days brought more examples of official severity. Smith's clerks were arrested as they came to work next morning, and though they were released after questioning, the store was kept under military guard. Since all the business books and papers had been taken, the prosperous firm of Smith Brothers and Company, the fruit of twenty years' hard work, had to close its doors. When Smith's family and friends tried to provide bail for him, they were told at first that no bail would be accepted. Then no one in Boston could be found with authority to take bail. Finally bail was set—at the outrageously high sum of $500,000. Yet so solid was Smith's reputation among Boston merchants that this huge amount and more—in all, about a million dollars—was pledged within two days. Still Smith was held incommunicado, denied counsel, his every letter censored. On June 23 almost the whole Massachusetts delegation to Congress called in a body on Secretary of the Navy Gideon Welles and offered to be personally responsible for Smith's appearance in court. But it was not until July 1, fourteen days after his arrest, that Smith was finally released. Still no specific charges had been lodged, but the bail had by this time been reduced to twenty thousand dollars.

Smith's troubles had just begun. The pretense for his arrest had been a vague allegation of "fraud upon the United States" in connection with contracts for naval hardware and "wilful neglect of duty as a contractor" with the Navy Department. But instead of being remanded for civil trial in United States federal court, Smith, though a civilian, was ordered to report for criminal trial to a naval general court-martial sitting in Philadelphia, far away from his home, his witnesses, his means of defense. Again the Massachusetts senators and representatives stepped in. Obtaining no satisfaction from Secretary Welles, they appealed over his head to President Lincoln. When Lincoln read the memorial that Senator Charles Sumner had drawn up and the others had signed, and when he had looked over the testimonial to Smith's business integrity, subscribed to by ninety prominent merchants of the Boston area, he proposed to quash the whole case.

"I believe a great injustice is being done to that man," said the President (according to a secondhand account published long afterward in the Boston *Herald*), "and I will put a stop to it at once."

By CURTIS DAHL

"Mr. President," said Senator Sumner (or Senator Henry Wilson—accounts differ), "we trust you will do nothing of the sort. To do that would be to leave a stigma on a good man's name. Smith Brothers want it never to be said that this charge was fixed up through influence. They challenge the fight but want protection against a conspiracy and a court chosen by their enemies. We only come to ask you that when the court convicts, as it is evident it means to do, you will personally review the case."

Lincoln agreed. "If I find that men have been pursuing the Smiths," he added, "I will lay my long hand upon them, no matter who they are."

Lincoln also ordered the court-martial shifted to Boston. "We don't have the money," Secretary Welles is supposed to have objected. "I guess you can find some," the President answered tersely. Welles considered his chief "sadly imposed upon by the cunning Bostonians."

The trial lasted from September 15, 1864, to January 13, 1865. Twice Smith broke down under the strain. On the 115th day the court reached the expected verdict: guilty. Smith was sentenced to a fine of twenty thousand dollars and imprisonment for two years.

What had Franklin W. Smith done to deserve such harsh treatment? Had he been an ordinary criminal, his case would be of only passing interest. If he had really been one of the host of dishonest contractors that preyed so voraciously on the Army and Navy during the Civil War, the hardships inflicted on him could be written off as one of those regrettable invasions of individual rights almost inevitable amid the hysteria of wartime. But what is shocking in the Smith case is that there seems to have been, if not a definite conspiracy, at least an unspoken agreement among certain officials of the Navy Department to "get" Smith. He was, it would seem, framed.

Franklin W. Smith, though a keen businessman, was at heart (as his later career abundantly proved) an idealist and reformer. When he saw wrong being done, he could not remain silent. The animus against him in the Navy Department arose from his repeated and well-documented charges that officials of Navy bureaus were conspiring with dishonest contractors to defraud the government through exorbitant prices and to throw all business to a favored "ring." As early as 1861 Smith had protested the laxity of the rules governing the reception and opening of contractors' bids and had forced reforms on unwilling bureau hands. Later he had reported to the authorities that an inspector at the Charlestown Navy Yard had offered to collude with a manufacturer of emery paper. In 1863 he had written to the chairman of the House Naval Affairs Committee and had appeared

Charlestown Navy Yard, where the trouble started
CULVER

before the corresponding committee of the Senate. Largely through Smith's efforts a law was passed on March 3, 1863, attempting to make bidding easier for honest contractors and manipulation harder for dishonest ones. In June of the same year Smith had named names of Navy clerks who had received bribes, and had written for Secretary Welles an "Analysis of Certain Contracts," showing definitely that help from inside the Navy Department must have been given to certain contractors to enable them so consistently to make the lowest bids.

The officers in the naval bureaus, whether guilty or not (and probably the chiefs themselves had clean hands), were naturally irked by a civilian's—and what was worse, a contractor's—sniping at their integrity. They were further chagrined by Smith's successful appearances before congressional committees and his habit of publishing each new charge in a privately printed pamphlet and circulating it as widely as possible. Hence, instead of seriously attempting to remove abuses in their own offices, they pursued the easier course of making countercharge after countercharge against the honesty of Smith Brothers and Company. Every possible pretext—a mistake in a bill, a delivery of unsatisfactory boiler plate, a copyist's error—was seized upon to discredit the firm. Yet always Smith produced exasperatingly convincing explanations and, when the charges were sifted, was consistently exonerated, at least once by Secretary Welles himself. Perhaps the greatest humiliation of all for the officers occurred when the Secretary circulated copies of one of Smith's pamphlets among the various bureau chiefs and required each one to prepare an answer to it. In doing so they almost wholly ignored the pamphlet's charges but fumed hotly against its "meddling" author.

The conflict did not remain a mere war of pamphlets. As a result of Smith's disclosures, a select committee of the Senate was appointed in January, 1864, to investigate frauds in naval contracts. It was under the chairmanship of fiery Senator John Parker Hale of New Hampshire, long a foe of the Navy Department. Years before, he had horrified the admirals by persuading Congress to abolish two hoary Navy customs: flogging and the regular issuance of a grog ration. He was later to lose his Senate seat partly because of the animosities aroused in the Smith case.

The Hale committee turned up convincing evidence that clerks in the naval bureaus had indeed been in cahoots with contractors. During the extended hearings, which lasted from February 11 to June 2, Smith and his brother were the principal witnesses against the Navy Department. The committee's majority report, submitted to the Senate on June 29, upheld the Smiths' charges and dismissed as unfounded the department's bitter allegations against them. Two weeks after the end of the hearings, even before the report had been made, the Smiths were arrested. One doubts whether this timing was coincidental: hurrying the two men off to Fort Warren was as good a way as any of discrediting the committee's report in advance.

What, specifically, were the accusations against Smith? And how true were they? Where there was so much smoke, was there no fire?

Specifically, the Smiths were charged with having supplied the Navy with Revely tin instead of a slightly more expensive type known as Banca, with machine-made instead of handmade files, with second- or third- rather than first-grade assorted hardware, with Stedman's emery paper instead of Sibley's (a slightly better grade), and with rusty, broken secondhand anchors instead of new ones. They were also accused of having fraudulently dissuaded another contractor from bidding to supply iron. But these were mere details—the handles by which the Navy Department's investigators hoped to get hold of Smith's papers, in which the investigators expected to find proof for the principal indictment: that Franklin Smith himself was in criminal collusion with Eugene L. Norton, Navy agent at Boston, and Matthew Merriam, chief machinist at the Charlestown Navy Yard. But unfortunately for the department its detectives, though they had investigated for over nine months and had been able to search through all Franklin Smith's books and personal letters, were not able to find enough evidence even to charge formally, much less to prove, collusion. Embarrassed, the Navy Department was left with only the lesser charges.

During the four weary months of the trial Smith was able to refute many of these. His expert witnesses defended the quality of his hardware. He showed that the prosecution could not definitely prove that certain allegedly defective articles had actually been delivered by Smith Brothers and Company. He argued convincingly that the supposedly incriminating letter about bidding for iron had been maliciously distorted by the prosecution's interpretation. But these matters of fact were really unimportant. Smith was entirely willing to admit, for instance, that he had delivered Revely tin on a contract specifying Banca and that a dozen or so of the 12,554

Franklin W. Smith, who blended business acumen with a zeal for reform, found a strong ally when a Navy clique sought his ruin.

articles delivered on a contract for assorted hardware might have been defective. What was important was the matter of fraudulent intent.

Smith utterly denied that he had ever knowingly or purposely defrauded the government or that he had been guilty of "wilful neglect of duty." He showed that his profits had by no means been excessive—they had averaged only about 5 per cent after store expenses. He proved that in the delivery of the tin he had merely followed common mercantile practice (the two kinds of tin were for all practical purposes interchangeable) and a long-standing arrangement with the Yard commandant. Furthermore, he had billed the government for Revely, not for Banca. How could fraud have been intended when it would gain Smith nothing? Again, in a time of great shortages defective articles of hardware were bound to appear. But had not Smith always been willing, often at considerable inconvenience and expense, to exchange anything found unsatisfactory? This was hardly criminal fraud.

Quite apart from the specific charges was the continuing insinuation by the prosecution that Smith, Norton, and Merriam were conspiring to overcharge the Navy. As evidence it was pointed out that a very large proportion of the Boston Navy Yard's hardware purchases was made from Smith Brothers and Company and the prices charged often averaged higher than the usual market

Executive Mansion.

Washington, Jan. 26. 186 5.

Hon. Secretary of the Navy

My dear Sir

I now understand that the record of the trial of Smith's brother at Boston is before you — Please do not let any execution of sentence take place, until the record shall have been before me.

Yours truly

A Lincoln

This letter from President Lincoln halted the persistent effort to destroy Smith, who a little later won complete vindication.

price. But here again Smith's rejoinder was convincing. Smith Brothers performed a real service to the Yard by specializing in obtaining the supplies of hardware it demanded when hardware and iron were exceedingly difficult to find. Thus, instead of being obliged to go to the almost impossible task of personally searching out the original makers of or special dealers for hundreds of different items, the Navy agent could leave that labor to Smith. Because Smith was acting as a middleman, he necessarily and justly charged slightly more than the regular market price.

As he had promised when the delegation of Smith's friends had presented their memorial to him, Lincoln requested Secretary Welles to send him the trial record and to postpone execution of the sentence until he had had an opportunity to review it. On February 22, 1865, Welles reluctantly sent to the White House the opinion written four days earlier by Charles Eames, counsellor of the Navy Department. Even Eames had been obliged to advise Welles that several of the specifications were not really proved and to urge mitigation of sentence. On March 13, having read every word of the papers, the President handed them to his close friend Sumner for his opinion. The senator's summary was succinct and strong. "To charge fraud against the respondents in this case," it went in part, "is cruel, irrational, preposterous. Their conduct cannot be tortured or twisted into fraud. As well

undertake to extract sunbeams out of cucumbers, or oil out of Massachusetts granite." Not only should the findings be set aside, Sumner continued, but positive restitution should be made.

According to the Boston *Herald*'s probably somewhat fanciful account, at five o'clock of the afternoon of March 17, 1865, President Lincoln was sitting in his carriage under the portico of the White House, waiting, as many another husband has, for his wife to come down for their usual afternoon drive. Suddenly, from his house directly across Lafayette Square appeared Charles Sumner, waving a sheaf of papers in his hand. He was angry as only a righteous man can be at a flagrant injustice. Putting his foot on the hub of the carriage wheel, he "poured out an eloquent torrent of denunciation" that ceased only at the appearance of Mrs. Lincoln.

"Come, Sumner," said the President, "that speech is too good to be lost. Get in here and take a ride with us."

Sumner climbed in. Off they went through the Washington streets, the senator declaiming all the way his belief that Franklin W. Smith was innocent. He had been railroaded. The gravest and most despicable injustice had been done. The President must act.

Before the trio had returned to the White House, Lincoln was fully convinced. "Come around in the morning," he said, "and I'll fix this up."

"No, Mr. President," Sumner is supposed to have replied, rising to his feet in the carriage, "you must not sleep until you have righted this wrong."

"Very well," was the slightly weary answer. "I have engagements after dinner until ten o'clock, but come then and we'll finish this up."

That night, in a driving thunderstorm, Sumner again crossed the square to the White House. Lincoln was at last alone. The senator went over the case with him until twenty minutes after midnight. Lincoln promised that before he went to bed he would write his decision; Sumner could have it in the morning.

At 9 A.M. the next day Sumner was ushered into the President's office. Lincoln turned to his friend and began to read his endorsement on the Smith case. Sumner had pointed out that in his opinion only the charge concerning the tin was at all convincing and that even if one assumed fraudulent intent, Smith could have gained at most only two hundred dollars on the transaction. But it was Lincoln who with the shrewd common sense of a country lawyer pierced through more than three thousand pages of the record's verbiage to the real heart of the matter. His endorsement cut through the prosecution's house of cards like the stroke of a sharp sword:

I am unwilling for the sentence to stand, and be executed, to any extent, in this case. In the absence of a more adequate motive than the evidence discloses, I am wholly unable to believe in the existence of criminal or fraudulent intent on the part of one of such well established good character, as is the accused. If the evidence went so far to establish a guilty profit of one or two hundred thousand dollars, as it does of one or two hundred dollars, this case would, on the question of guilt, bear a far different aspect. That on this contract, involving from one million to twelve hundred thousand dollars, the contractors should attempt a fraud which at the most could profit them only one or two hundred, or even one thousand dollars, is to my mind beyond the power of rational belief. That they did not, in such a case, strike for greater gains proves that they did not, with guilty, or fraudulent intent, strike at all. Judgment and sentence are disapproved, and declared null, and the accused ordered to be discharged.

After all the months of persecution, Franklin W. Smith, the would-be reformer, was cleared. He had found a judge who, acting not in mercy but in plain justice, saw the simple truth lying clouded in the thousands of pages of court testimony and declamation. Smith was wholly exonerated, the case expunged from the beginning.

The heartwarming drama of Lincoln as the white knight rescuing the idealist Mr. Smith from the toils of dark conspiracy should not, however, obscure several larger issues inherent in the Smith case. For these issues are still alive in America today.

When Senator Wilson of Massachusetts, a friend of Smith's, called the case to Lincoln's attention, the President is supposed to have said: "I know all about it, Wilson; it is a fight between a department and a citizen, and the citizen has no fair show." In the best tradition of democracy Lincoln used his Presidential prerogative to uphold the rights of a private citizen against the massive power of a governmental agency—and a military department, in wartime, at that. But even more significant to us today is the fact that in quashing the conviction of Smith, Lincoln was protecting a man from retaliation for having testified as a witness before a congressional committee. Smith was being hounded largely because in his appearance before the select committee he had dared to point out corruption in the Navy Department. Had Lincoln not acted, the department would have succeeded in punishing and discrediting its most vocal critic.

An even larger issue was at stake: the power of Congress to suspend the constitutional rights of individual citizens. It was this aspect of the case that caused it to be debated fiercely in Congress. In bringing the Boston contractor to trial, the Navy Department was making use of an act of July 17, 1862, that stipulated that anyone contracting to supply material to the Army or Navy was by that fact alone a member of the armed forces and subject to trial by court-martial. In Smith's case, this law took from a government contractor, who in all other respects remained a civilian, his constitutional right to a hearing before a grand jury, to a trial in his home district by a jury of his peers, and to his right of habeas corpus. As the trial proceeded Smith's lawyers soon learned that the act of 1862 also deprived their client of the many safeguards of civilian law. If Congress by decree could withdraw constitutional rights from military and naval contractors, why could it not abolish them for any group? If it could, the Bill of Rights was a nullity.

A third vital issue inherent in the Smith case was that of civilian control of military departments. Gideon Welles, Secretary of the Navy, was a conscientious, law-abiding ex-newspaperman with great respect for individual rights. Sincere and well-intentioned though he was, he naturally had to rely for information and advice on his professional subordinates, particularly on Assistant Secretary Gustavus Vasa Fox, who as a veteran naval officer probably knew more about the Navy than his chief. The reluctant Welles had been persuaded by the vehemence of the angry professional officers led by Fox (whose bitterness against Smith was immeasurably increased by his intense personal and political hatred of Smith's defender, Senator Hale) to sanction Smith's arrest and trial. As his diary shows, the Secretary had gradually been convinced by Fox that the Smiths were the most brazen hypocrites. What the commissioned officers and their ally Fox wanted to do, they did. Though at the time Welles deeply resented the President's action, Lincoln's freeing of Smith actually redressed the balance toward civilian control.

The news of Lincoln's clearing of Smith, telegraphed by Sumner, was received with jubilation in Boston. Sumner was deluged with letters praising him for his part in the case, Smith with messages of congratulation from all over the nation. After a thorough and painstaking investigation of the whole case the Boston Board of Trade completely exonerated Smith and reinstated him as a director. The press, in both Boston and New York, had been almost uniformly on Smith's side during the trial; now it acclaimed the President's act. In 1866, ruling on a similar case, a federal circuit court in Kentucky declared unconstitutional the act of July 17, 1862, under which Smith had been tried. But perhaps Smith's greatest victory came on April 15, 1865, when a great crowd of Bostonians gathered in Tremont Temple to mourn the tragic death of Lincoln. Feeling that no other would so deeply and honorably regret Lincoln's passing, Smith's neighbors unanimously chose him to preside over their meeting.

Curtis Dahl, Samuel Valentine Cole Professor of English Literature at Wheaton College, in Norton, Massachusetts, is a previous contributor and the author of several critical works on American literature.

Typical payoff of an election bet as depicted by an artist in 1908

The Melancholy Fate of the Loser

By GERALD CARSON

It isn't every day that one can see a man pushing a peanut with his nose along the main street of an American town. But it is not an impossible sight, either, especially when election wagers are being settled after what ex-President Truman has called our "four-yearly spasm." Sometimes the penance is performed with an orange or golf ball. Or the loser transports the winner over an agreed-upon route in a baby carriage or handcart. Losers have gamely walked barefoot, been rotten-egged, eaten crow—literally—for their fallible political judgment. But the long-time favorite of all zany arrangements of this sort requires a wheelbarrow. Meet, then, the man who started it all, Major Ben: Perley Poore (that's the way he wrote his name), who introduced wheelbarrow trundling into the Presidential canvass shortly before the Civil War. More blithe spirit than party zealot,

In 1856 journalist Poore bet on Millard Fillmore. He paid off by pushing a barrel of apples 36 miles.

Reuel Gridley, grocer, with a sack of flour that not only paid a bet in a Nevada mining camp but also raised $275,000 for Union soldiers' relief.

Edward Payson Weston walked all the way from Boston to Washington in 1861 because he thought Lincoln would lose.

Every Sunday for six months Martin Winkowski had to shine his brother's shoes. The sign he wears explains why.

Poore was a Massachusetts militia officer, a jovial companion, and a successful journalist in Washington, and sometimes called the first American political columnist. During a visit to his ancestral home at West Newbury, Massachusetts, in June, 1856, Major Poore vowed that ex-President Millard Fillmore would beat John C. Frémont in the Republican primaries of his home state. His friend Robert I. Burbank, lawyer, state senator, and colonel of the 1st Regiment, Massachusetts Volunteer Militia, held the opposite opinion, and a wager was arranged. The terms: the loser would present a barrel of apples to the winner and personally propel the barrel in a wheelbarrow from his own home to the residence of the winner.

In the November election Fillmore ran poorly, polling less than 20,000 votes to Frémont's 100,000-plus. Major Poore immediately prepared to pay up. Burbank lived at the swanky Tremont House in Boston, the first "palace" hotel in the United States. It was thirty-six-and-a-quarter miles from Major Poore's "Indian Hill" estate. Colonel Burbank offered to release the major from his bet, ending a gracious note to that effect with "Yours, for Frémont, Freedom and the rise of real estate in Kansas." Poore refused the soft option, signing himself in reply, "Yours for Fillmore and the Constitution," and appending two postscripts: "I shall be very *dry* when I get to the Tremont House" and "Kansas be d————d."

Harnessed to his one-wheeler by a strap crossed over his shoulders, Major Poore pushed the 185-pound load of King apples, fall sweet apples, and quinces to Boston in a little more than two working, or walking, days. At the Charlestown bridge the major, shoulders blackened by his straps and hands blistered by the wheelbarrow handles, his own weight down by twelve pounds, was met by an enthusiastic body of Fillmore admirers, the Boston Cornet Band, the Independent Fusiliers, and two daguerreotypists. Major Poore marched in the middle of the procession, his wheelbarrow decorated with the American flag and a banner bearing the legend "Maj. Poore—may the next administration prove as faithful to their pledges as he was to his."

A cheering crowd filled State, Court, and Washington streets. When the cortege reached the hotel, the barrel was upended under the portico. Standing on the impromptu platform, Colonel Burbank saluted Major Poore as a noble pioneer: "You have had the fortune to introduce in political *tactics* a new method of *wheeling*," and declared the wheelbarrow was "already . . . a chariot of Fame." The two patriots then entered the parlors of the Tremont House, and the colonel asked the major what he would take to cure his dryness.

Ever since this exploit, the wheelbarrow has been the principal vehicle for bizarre wagers on the Presidency. In 1892, for instance, happy Democrats in New York's Fourth Ward gathered for a victory celebration at Sulzer's oasis on Henry Street to see Charles W. Ahearn, who did not believe that Grover Cleveland could be elected, pay for his error. Wearing a tall "grandfather's" hat swathed in the American flag, Ahearn conveyed Timothy P. Bourke past the newspaper offices that then lined Park Row. In a wheelbarrow, of course. Bourke held a flag in each hand and reclined upon two luxurious pillows.

Whimsical costumes are generally added to the central concept of the wheelbarrow. Kansans seem to have a special gift for developing this extra twist. Charles Nichols put on bright red underwear in 1936 when he wheeled *two* winners through the business district of Independence, while Charles Taylor, then director of the state Chamber of Commerce, gave a prominent businessman of

Liberal, Kansas, a free ride, pushing the conveyance while clad in a woman's housedress and slippers.

Other imaginative efforts to propitiate Lady Luck have included a pledge to read 121 consecutive issues of the editorial page of the New York *Tribune*, a form of punishment that the rival *Times* denounced as inhumane. In the Cleveland-Blaine contest of 1884, the year in which the leading orator of the Gilded Age, Colonel Robert G. Ingersoll, eulogized James G. Blaine as a "plumed knight," a Blaine stalwart, having lost his bet, was required to get into a suit of armor, don a helmet, put on a shirt of chain mail, and wear a plume for thirty days. It was a tough year for knights.

To return to more recent times, a Chicago man found after the quadrennial fever subsided on November 4, 1948, that he had to shine his brother's shoes every Sunday morning for six months. Furthermore, the penitential act had to be performed in public, at Milwaukee and Damen avenues, under a sign that announced: "I voted for Dewey."

There have been a good many walkers. The first was Edward Payson Weston, who walked so well that he turned professional. Weston agreed to walk from the State House in Boston to the Capitol in Washington in ten consecutive days if Stephen A. Douglas lost to Abraham Lincoln. This he did on November 6, 1860. Under the terms of the bet "Payse" Weston had to start out on February 22, 1861, and make it to the Capitol in time for Lincoln's inauguration. The walker touched the cornerstone of the building in the late afternoon of March 4, a few hours after the ceremony. Even so, the stunt was so remarkable that the next day the *Evening Star* paid more attention to Weston's movements than it did to Lincoln's.

One offbeat wager accomplished an astonishing amount of practical good. It took place in 1864 in the

rough mining camp of Austin, Nevada. The occasion was the choice of a mayor. The election had, however, a larger significance because of the tensions of the Civil War. Reuel Gridley, the town grocer, backed a Southern Democrat's candidacy with a sack of flour. "If I lose," he said, "I'll carry the sack a mile to Clifton and back again to the tune of 'John Brown's Body.' And if you lose," Gridley told Dr. Herrick, who voted Republican, "you carry it to the tune of 'Dixie.' "

The Republican candidate won, and Gridley fulfilled his pledge, accompanied by thirty-six men on horseback, the town fathers, and a brass band. Later, at a local saloon, the idea was hatched of auctioning the sack of flour for the benefit of the sick and wounded soldiers of the Union Army. The auction was held, producing over five thousand dollars in mining stock, town lots, and cash. It was followed by similar vendues all over Washoe County. The sack of flour was carried triumphantly to Sacramento and San Francisco and finally reached New York, earning a total of $275,000 for the Sanitary Commission. The original flour bag, neatly repaired, still exists among the treasured artifacts of the Nevada Historical Society.

Major Poore certainly started something, for unless tradition fails, political flagellation will again crop up in the news after November, 1972, including, no doubt, wheelbarrow pushing. "One may have a hope, a belief, or an opinion," Francis Bacon, the Lord Chancellor of England, wrote in the seventeenth century, "but unless he bets he can have no certainty." Bacon, alas, raised false hopes, since there must always be a loser for every winner.

A regular contributor to AMERICAN HERITAGE, *Gerald Carson has not one but two wheelbarrows at his home in Millerton, New York, but no plans to use them next month.*

In the year 1854 a young man named George Washington Eastman rather reluctantly maintained a residence in Waterville, New York. The reluctance arose from the fact that while the hamlet was pleasant enough, its population of a few hundred souls offered no scope for the ambitions and needs of a father of two little girls, with a third child on the way. George Washington Eastman was a teacher of the arts of business, and to find pupils he was obliged to leave his wife Maria, and little Ellen and Emma, for regular trips to Roches-

Wholesale, Retail, Commission, Banking, Manufacturing, Shipping and Steam-Boating, Individual Partnership and Compound Company Business." The cost—diploma included—was twenty-five dollars. An extra five allowed students to take the "teacher's course," which included "Ornamental Penmanship in all the Ancient and Modern Hands."

On July 12, 1854, the new baby—a son, named George—was born. Six

eration of entrepreneurs who transformed the United States into a twentieth-century society. For George Eastman belongs on the muster roll of capitalists whose specialty was to wed the scientific discoveries of the nineteenth century to mass-producing and marketing techniques, and thereby to create enormous quantities of goods for Everyman. They made the consumer king, and like court necromancers won favor by providing royalty with comforts, gadgets, and diversions. Like Thomas Edison or Alexander Graham Bell or

"You Press the Button, We Do the Rest"

To show how easy it was to use a Kodak, the boy at left posed two of his chums at the Genesee Gorge in upstate New York, about 1890.

BOTH: U.P.I.

ter, some seventy miles to the west. As a busy stop on the Erie Canal and a flour-milling center with other growing industries, Rochester furnished a supply of young men to enroll in Eastman's Commercial College, which he opened there to instruct them in "Commercial Penmanship and Book-Keeping by Double Entry," as used in all branches of "Trade and Commerce, Including

years after that the hard-working father moved the family to Rochester and finally eliminated his back-and-forth journeyings. Two years later he died. It is a pity that George Washington Eastman, professor of business, did not live to see his son grow up to become a master of wholesale, retail, manufacturing, and "compound company" affairs—one of the top dozen or so among a gen-

Henry Ford—to name but a few—Eastman was able to combine his own hunches, his grasp of theory, and other men's ideas in sharply focused inventions that had immediate, practical, common utility. Like them, too, he was able to orchestrate the work of engineering and merchandising experts so as to put the invented device into the hands of millions.

By BERNARD A. WEISBERGER

His presentation to mankind was the inexpensive, popular camera. At first glance it may seem an instrument of much less social gravity and consequence than the electric light, the telephone, or the automobile. But it is worth recollecting that the camera, joined with electric lights and motors (in inventions by Edison), created the movies; that the camera, crossed with the electron gun, is responsible for television. In a certain sense Eastman carries the awesome paternity of the modern age of the image, with all its deep effects on man's consciousness and sense of reality.

His childhood and youth seemed commonplace enough, though they were given something of a harsh edge by economic adversity. George Washington Eastman's death left his widow almost penniless. She kept things going by taking in boarders, and the children grew up watching her struggle bitterly with the chores of housekeeping on a pinched budget. George adored his mother and swore from the start that he would repay her for her efforts and sacrifices some day. It became a lodestar in his life.

Still it was not a bad childhood. Young America liked to think of its future heroes as having been specifically toughened by the tasks of frontier farming. But Eastman was a city boy who never split a rail or hunted for the family's supper. He was a quiet, undistinguished schoolboy, on the whole seemingly more given to prudence than to pranks. He had a knack for tinkering, and likewise a strong attachment to capitalist economics, at an early age. Once he constructed an ingenious puzzle out of wires. An admiring friend asked for it as a gift, but young George demanded, and got, cash on the barrelhead—reputedly ten cents.

At fourteen, like most of his self-sufficient peers, Eastman went forth to wrestle with the world, his formal schooling done. He found a job as an office boy in an insurance company.

Though his initial tasks included such lowly assignments as cleaning the boss's cuspidor, he worked his way steadily upward to clerk. Later he became a junior officer in a bank. His salary began at three dollars a week. By the time he was in his early twenties, the bank was paying him a then very comfortable fourteen hundred a year.

From the start he showed a great sense of the value of a dollar, an instinct for organization, a gift for

George Eastman, a formal pose taken in Paris in 1890 by the photographer Nadar

management. He began to keep a pocket notebook, meticulously recording his expenses to the penny. Though the entries showed the profile of a careful young man, Eastman was not entirely dedicated to work and money. Along with the notations of expenditures for clothes, meals, and other necessities there

were items for candy, visits to places of scenic or historic interest, horseback rides, shooting galleries, and other moderately frivolous diversions. He enjoyed leisure; in fact in later life he was to insist that he did not really like to work. And he made the appropriate moves in the direction of self-improvement expected of a young man in that era of high seriousness. He bought a flute and books in French, though whether he got very far in learning to use either of these marks of cultivation is not clear. He bought dumbbells to help develop his muscles. Nor did he seem neglectful of growth in a social direction. Some of his expenditures were for ice cream and other treats for girls whom he took out on the rounds of Rochester's pleasures. But he formed no serious attachment to any single one—his notebook records his escorting three different girls, at various times, to one of the town's chief attractions, the roof of the seven-story-high Powers Building. Nor did his dates diminish his attachment to his mother. He was prolific with small gifts for her, and from her shoulders he took an increasing load of responsibility as he grew older —ordering furniture and carpets, supervising spring cleaning, and in other ways acting as head of the household. But for all these expenditures, outgo was carefully kept below income, and at each year's end a banked surplus of earnings was entered in the account book. Later some of this reserve would go into interest-bearing bonds, real estate, and other enterprises that happily illustrated the breeding properties of money properly laid out.

He seemed methodical, and perhaps a touch dull. It was not simply a question of respectability, but of style. Things had to be complete and in order. In 1876, for example, he treated himself to a trip to Philadelphia to see the Centennial Exposition. "Today," he wrote to his mother, "I finished the Machinery Hall and

The 1888 Kodak and leather case

Eastman with Edison, 1928

A typical advertisement, ca. 1888

Kodak advertising methods, including the famous-man endorsement, were advanced for the time.

some small buildings, and about halfway across the end aisle of the Main." The results of this dutiful touristic pilgrimage were interesting; the machinery was "bewildering" to him, but he admired the "ingenuity that exhibitors have displayed in arranging . . . apparently uninteresting articles."

Arrangements always beguiled him. In later life, on camping and hunting trips that became favorite pastimes, he delighted in supervising the packing and in concocting intricate nests of boxes to protect fragile contents, or dividing supplies into parcels of exactly equal weight so that pack animals could be given identical loads. The quest for efficiency also showed in his domestic arrangements. He devised premeasured packages of cake and bread mixes to carry on his safaris long before they were marketed commercially; he triumphantly announced to friends in 1882 his discovery of a way to filter coffee grounds by pouring the boiled coffee through absorbent cotton. He was an inveterate gadgeteer.

One would have tabbed him for possible success—but in a carefully circumscribed and unadventurous field. Older, knowing associates might have predicted that he would become a banker and a spare-time creative hobbyist. The odds on his dealing in a product whose commercial career would require innovation and risk seemed low, if one examined his patterns up to 1877. But then photography entered and transformed George Eastman's life.

It began simply enough. In 1877 he planned on a vacation trip to Santo Domingo, then in the news because of recent American interest in annexing it or at least establishing a naval base there. One of Eastman's friends at the bank had been a photographer on the expedition led by John Wesley Powell that explored the canyons of the Colorado River. He suggested to George that a pho-

tographic record of his Caribbean excursion would be well worth having. Nothing loath, Eastman plunged in—and the plunge was a deep one. The trip never materialized, but Eastman was committed to the new art from the beginning. The first step was a heavy investment in equipment. In later years he wrote that when he began as a photographer, one did not take a camera on a trip, one "accompanied an outfit of which the camera was only a part."

The process then used was wetplate photography, in which the image was recorded on glass plates coated with a light-sensitive emulsion. It was necessary to prepare the plates immediately before use and expose and develop them before they dried. To achieve this a formidable amount of gear was required. Eastman's initial purchases—the bill of sale for which he carefully preserved —came to over fifty dollars, a goodly sum in 1877, and subsequent acquisitions raised his opening investment in the art to more than ninety dollars, which possibly did not include the five he paid someone for lessons. The starting kit included not only the heavy camera itself, together with a tripod, plus plates, paper, boxes for storing negatives, and a tent that could be set up as a darkroom, but also the furnishings of a small chemistry laboratory—nitrate of silver, acetate soda, chlorides of gold, sodium, and iron, collodion, varnish, alcohol, litmus paper, hydrometer, graduate, evaporating dish, funnel, bristle brush, scales and weights, and washing pans. All of this had to be packed along to the site of the picture taking, which therefore became a hobby only for the affluent and for the extraordinarily patient and dedicated.

It would become Eastman's fate to change all this. The mysterious internal process that drew him at once to become deeply involved with the camera is beyond the historian's probe. It is enough to say that the young bank clerk began to spend increasing amounts of time behind the lens and in the developing room, and to read everything he could lay hands on concerning photographic techniques. At some point his pastime began to demand a share of his energy that could have encroached on his business career if he had not decided to make his pastime his business. This turning point was reached some time in 1878. Later on—perhaps with the benefit of hindsight—Eastman expressed a philosophy that explained the development of his career. Though he enjoyed reading about science, he declared in a magazine article written when he was nearly sixty, the intellectual adventure of pure research was not fulfilling. "There is, to me," he said, "more adventure in putting each discovery to the ultimate test of public use, for then the discovery becomes an addition to everyday life." If this was, in fact, a belief that he held at twenty-four, it explains why he moved quickly toward making photography more efficient and more available to others.

Eastman's first interest, like that of other photographers at the time, was in devising a dry plate, which would eliminate the awkward need for immediate development of a shot. The problem was to find an emulsion that would keep its sensitivity even when dried and held in storage. In the journals of photography, both British and American, to which Eastman subscribed, enthusiastic amateurs exchanged recipes for such emulsions like gourmet cooks. He himself joined zealously in the quest. He continued to work at the bank by day, but at night he would return to the rented house faithfully kept by his mother, eat supper, then go into the kitchen to measure, pour, stir, and test for hours on end. He had great powers of concentration. Often he would remain at this task overnight, and when this proved too taxing, he set up a cot so that he could

fall upon it, fully dressed, for restorative naps. A youthful constitution buoyed him through these rigors, and by 1880 he had invented and patented not only a dry plate but a machine for preparing large numbers of such plates quickly. The basis of his process—not the only one on the market, to be sure—was an emulsion containing gelatin, which when dried adequately protected the sensitized surface against the hard knocks of shipment and usage.

Now he vaulted into the world of self-employment. He had his patents, he had three thousand dollars in savings, and to strengthen his hand he took a partner. One of his mother's boarders had been Henry A. Strong, a likable manufacturer of buggy whips who had grown attached to Eastman and who would one day write him: "You are a queer cuss, Geo., . . . but I want you to know . . . that I am always with you heart and hand. Never take my silence for indifference. . . . We surely are neither of us very demonstrative."

Undemonstrative or not, Strong had enough faith in his young friend to join him in renting one floor of a factory building and commencing the operations of the Eastman Dry Plate Company, which officially went into business on New Year's Day, 1881.

The first year was sweaty and successful. No longer the leisure-loving young bachelor, Eastman worked with incredible energy at finding jobbers and customers, publicizing the firm, overseeing the physical details of production—and improving the product. He would not rest content with merely an entry into a branch of the photographic-supply business. "The idea gradually dawned on me," he recollected later, "that what we were doing . . . was not merely making dry plates, but that we were starting out to make photography an everyday affair." Or, as he afterward put it more crisply, to "make the camera as con-

Eastman en route to Europe, 1890

The Rochester factory, 1890

Processing prints by exposure to sunlight

Partner Henry A. Strong dictates a letter.

Eastman on a camping trip in Canada in 1912

venient as the pencil."

There were ups and downs. In the first three months the firm got enough orders to occupy six employees. And before the end of 1881 the company was in larger quarters, in a four-story building on State Street, Rochester's major downtown thoroughfare. Eastman had also gone abroad, found dealers, and set up offices in England. But then disaster almost overwhelmed him. Reports came back to Rochester from across the Atlantic: plate after plate made by the firm had turned out defective.

Eastman met the crisis with dispatch. He set associates to work around the clock checking factory operations to see what was going wrong, and immediately took ship for England to examine the defective stock. He then, figuratively, took a deep breath and sent a message to every customer: each and every bad plate would be replaced without charge. There was no way of knowing the extent of this commitment when it was made. For all Eastman knew, his entire product for months might have been useless. As it turned out, however, only a single batch of emulsion had gone bad, and only a limited number of plates had slowly deteriorated on wholesalers' and shopkeepers' shelves. Eastman emerged from the episode with a solid reputation for standing behind his product.

By early 1883 the bit was in his teeth. He wanted to go beyond dry plates, which were still, after all, fragile and space-consuming sheets of treated glass. Photographers were now looking for something else—a material that would be lightweight, flexible, easily stored (perhaps in the camera itself), and durable—a "film" on which images could be captured, to be printed later.

Eastman did not conceive of the idea of film on his own. He was not the first or last man to experiment with an eye to creating it, and some of his company's basic patents were discovered by others and only purchased by him. (At least one inventor claimed priority on a fundamental Eastman process, and won his lawsuit.) Yet Eastman was the persistent, determined leader who put the power of organization and capital into the quest. It had taken him but five years—1878 to 1883—to move from amateur picture taking to success as a manufacturer of equipment that made life easier for thousands of other amateurs. In just the next five years he would move most of the remaining distance toward the goal of a camera "as convenient as the pencil."

Film was the key innovation. The problem was to find a substance that could be produced in a continuous strip—like a set of dry plates joined together—drawn past the lens, and subjected to the handling that would turn exposures into prints without stretching and tearing. The first result achieved by Eastman and his coworkers was an emulsion containing collodion, which was a solution of nitrocellulose in ether and alcohol that dried to a tough film and had been used to coat plates and in other photographic applications since the early days of the art. (It was also esteemed by doctors for holding dressings in place and covering wounds and lesions.) This emulsion was spread on a strip of paper and dried. The paper, which provided the necessary tensile strength and spooling properties, was stripped away after exposure, and the film proper could then be processed successfully. In 1884 Eastman's company took out patents on this American Film, as he called it, and prepared for an assault on the market. He reorganized his firm under a new name, the Eastman Dry Plate and Film Company. Its capital was increased to $200,000. Half of that was the estimated value of the patents held by Strong, Eastman, and an associate named William H.

Walker, and half was new capital. The simple partnership of Eastman and Strong was on its way to becoming a major corporation. In 1885 a device called a roll holder—an attachment for any camera, which carried a supply of the paper-backed film—was patented.

The film and holder by themselves were important steps but not enough to guarantee the creation of a true mass market for cameras. There were handling problems that involved inexperienced users in disaster—most especially the stripping operation, during which the film often was pulled out of shape or hopelessly ripped. Eastman saw that what was needed was a "complete system" that could somehow be utilized by anyone, even a photographic ignoramus wholly unaware of the very definition of such words as "lens" and "negative" but simply anxious to have a picture of what he saw before him. The answer would lie in both a better film and a better camera.

While the quest for film was in progress, Eastman's plant, and others, had been working toward small and light cameras to replace the heavy, tripod-mounted instruments that, with their long bellows, were familiar in studios. A few box-shaped hand cameras were available early in the 1880's, and because they sometimes were unrecognizable as photographic equipment, they theoretically allowed subjects to be taken unawares. For this reason they were called detective cameras. Eastman designed and marketed one in 1886, but it ran into production difficulties. It was not fated, therefore, to be what he was really looking for—a camera "that would take pictures in the hands of a greenhorn."

In 1888 that camera was born. Into the world came Everyman's magic box for freezing moments of personal history into pictorial permanence. All in the wink of an eye, the click of a shutter, it could imprint a memory on a piece of paper for time unending. If photography itself was something of a miracle, this made the miracle instantaneous and almost anyone a miracle worker. The new camera bore a strange name, proudly worked out (and later explicated) by Eastman. "Kodak," he called it, because

a trademark should be short, vigorous, incapable of being misspelled to an extent that will destroy its identity and—in order to satisfy trademark laws—it must mean nothing. . . .

The letter "K" had been a favorite with me—it seems a strong, incisive sort of letter. Therefore, the word I wanted had to start with "K." Then it became a question of trying out a great number of combinations of letters that made words starting and ending with "K." The word Kodak is the result. Instead of merely making cameras and camera supplies, we made Kodaks and Kodak supplies. It became the distinctive word for our products. Hence the slogan: "If it isn't an Eastman, it isn't a Kodak."

It was a superb trade name; it had something of the snap of the lens-opening mechanism about it—something brisk and decisive. It was a near-palindrome, almost impossible to forget or misspell. And like "Victrola," "Thermos bottle," and "Scotch Tape"—all manufacturers' names for brands of record players, vacuum bottles, and cellophane tape —"Kodak," as Eastman desired and predicted, became the perfect trademark, a synonym for the product itself.

The primal Kodak—the Model T of cameradom—was compact by standards of that time. It was 6½ inches long, 3¼ wide, and 3¾ inches high. Made of wood, it had a fixed-focus lens. It could easily be carried in a leather case. The picture it took was round and a scant 2½ inches in diameter. And it cost twenty-five dollars. The owner was emancipated from any concern with even the simplest mechanics. The camera came already loaded with enough film for one hundred exposures. The shutter was snapped, a key wound to advance the film, and a string pulled to recock the shutter. And when the last photo was taken, the user simply sent the entire box back to Rochester. There Eastman's specially trained workers opened it, stripped the film, developed the shots, and returned to the sender his finished prints, and the camera, reloaded. This cost ten dollars, but it meant that once the initial cost was absorbed, a Kodak buyer was getting pictures at ten cents apiece. No matter how much of a duffer he was, moreover, if he could point the camera at a target in enough light, he could count on capturing the scene. Eastman's advertising slogan was not only inspired in being concise and personal but, unlike many such statements, was also literally true. It said, with majestic simplicity: "You press the button, we do the rest."

Eighteen eighty-eight was Kodak's birth year. Eighteen eighty-nine saw another major step. A chemist hired by Eastman, Henry Reichenbach, had been busily working for three years on a film that would not need any backing. Eastman was spurred on in the search by requests from Thomas Edison for something that he could use in the motion-picture camera he was developing. It would have to be tough enough to be perforated and whirled rapidly through sprocketed wheels, and it would have to be capable of being produced in great lengths.

Reichenbach built upon experimental foundations that had already been laid in treating collodion with various substances and that had resulted in the invention of celluloid in 1868. He finally found that a mixture of camphor, fusel oil, and amyl acetate, dissolved in a solution of nitrocellulose and wood alcohol, would dry to form a transparent negative film that needed no support from paper or anything else. The discovery not only opened the door to movie making but it emancipated even Kodak users from the extra step of returning their films to the plant for stripping and processing. The way was now open for development at home or, in time, at any of numerous photographic stores, and eventually corner drugstores. The new film was a crowning touch.

Reichenbach and Eastman did not know that almost simultaneously with their application for a patent for this new kind of roll film a New Jersey minister named Hannibal Goodwin had come up with an essentially similar invention. Goodwin lacked the funds to make the necessary tests, so he did not receive his patent for another eleven years. Eastman, on the other hand, was able to rush into the marketplace. Goodwin's patents later found their way into the hands of the Ansco Company, and in 1914, after lengthy litigation (and after Goodwin's death), a court ruled that Eastman had to pay Ansco five million dollars, despite his grumbling that "Mr. Goodwin never made a roll of film." By then Reichenbach had long since left the Eastman company—fired after a quarrel and the discovery that he was planning to set up a rival firm. So neither of the two inventors of film shared Eastman's later reputation as the true begetter of popular photography, a fame which he deserved, but more as promoter and manufacturer than as sole scientific discoverer.

The nineties opened, therefore, with the Kodak in existence—a simple box camera using flexible film, suitable for mass production, and achieved only twelve years after Eastman had first acquired for himself the cumbersome paraphernalia of photography. In his second decade as a businessman Eastman pyramided his firm into a multimillion-

A bachelor, Eastman was devoted to his mother, who is shown here on the porch of the house he purchased in Rochester in the 1890's. In 1905 mother and son moved to the palatial thirty-seven-room mansion he built, Eastman House, now the noted museum of photography.

growth in the nineties. Technology had produced newspaper presses capable of each day turning out hundreds of thousands of copies of newspapers containing dozens of pages. And in those pages there was ample display of illustrated appeals to buy the varied array of ready-made goods pouring out of the country's factories. Urbanites especially—a growing segment of the population—were steadily exposed to tempting pictures of boots and shoes, bonnets and corsets, patent medicines and packaged foods, rugs and furniture, watches and hardware, sewing and washing machines, baby buggies and pianos, stoves and so on, almost endlessly. In this world of huckstering Eastman moved with boldness and a brilliant sense of direction. In May of 1889 he took full-page advertisements in all the major magazines—*Harper's, Century, Scribner's, Harper's Weekly, Frank Leslie's, Puck, Judge,* and *Life*—to sing the praises of the new film (which he was convinced would "*entirely* replace glass plates, at least for amateur work . . . as fast as the goods can be made"). This campaign of magazine advertising was never relaxed, and its themes varied. The basic chord was "you press the button," but testimonials were solicited showing the variety of uses to which the Kodak could be put. A doctor's wife took pictures of patients' visible symptoms to assist her husband. A passenger agent of a railroad took shots of the scenery along the route and used them as display ads. Burton Holmes, a travel lecturer, naturally found the Kodak indispensable for bringing back evidence of the attractions he described.

The great were frequently cited as Kodak users; one advertisement noted that the wife of Chicago's traction magnate Charles Yerkes and likewise Mrs. George M. Pullman, whose husband manufactured the famous sleeping cars, "'press the button' of the Kodak with good results." It was, of course, an extra at-

dollar trust. He did so by a combination of techniques that would become familiar in other branches of industry. They included heavy advertising; a steady drive to control all the steps in the production process, from raw material to finished goods; a reach for monopoly; and relentless improvement and cheapening of the product. Kodak was a model for

what was going on elsewhere in American industry in those economically stormy and significant years. Modern America's tastes, habits, and industrial productive patterns were emerging, and Eastman's success came in part through his careful estimates of what their ultimate shape would be.

Advertising had ample room for

traction that even ladies, presumably daunted by anything mechanical, could easily work the camera. In England, Eastman got additional advertising leverage from celebrities. Prince George and Princess Mary (later King George V and his queen) were Kodak carriers. Rudyard Kipling was willing, one assumes for a consideration, to declare publicly that he was "amazed at the excellence of the little Kodak's work." In 1897 a huge electric sign flashed the Kodak name over Trafalgar Square. One somewhat spectacular plug was in a little-known Gilbert and Sullivan operetta, *Utopia*, which introduced two "modest maidens" who sang:

Then all the crowd take down our looks
In pocket memorandum books.
To diagnose
Our modest pose
The Kodaks do their best:
If evidence you would possess
Of what is maiden bashfulness,
You only need a button press—
And we will do the rest.

Such messages—and by 1899 Kodak's advertising budget was up to three quarters of a million dollars per year (as contrasted with forty-eight million in 1970)—found a ready audience because of a social development that was accelerating steadily as the old century died and the new replaced it. This was the increase in popular leisure and in activities to fill it. The period from 1890 to 1910 saw, among other things, the bicycle craze; the proliferation of outdoor hiking clubs; the beginnings of automobile tourism; the heyday of vaudeville; the early, crude movies; the development of baseball into a universally enjoyed spectator sport, with a network of major and minor leagues; the beginnings of big-time college football—it is possible to go on in a Whitmanesque fashion. Increasingly, Americans who lived above the poverty line took to diverting themselves,

and the camera was a perfect companion. Society was ready for the Kodak.

Eastman also prepared for the conquest of mass markets with a steady program of expansion, reorganization, and strategic control of all the avenues and byways of the picture business. At one point he wrote with enthusiasm to Strong: "The manifest destiny of the Eastman Kodak Company is to be the largest manufacturer of photographic materials in the world or go to pot." There was little chance of a journey potwards, however. A reorganization of the Eastman Dry Plate and Film Company in 1890 capitalized the corporation at a million dollars. In 1892 another session with bankers and lawyers resulted in the Eastman Kodak Company of New York, capital five million. In 1898 there was still another metamorphosis, and a new structure including Kodak, Ltd., a large British subsidiary, was set up, with a capitalization of eight million dollars. Eastman made a personal profit of $960,000 as the arranger of the reorganization and enjoyed reporting that when he elatedly told his mother: "Mother, we have a million dollars now," her sole comment was: "That's nice, George." By then materials-manufacturing centers had been set up in a number of countries, a new factory exclusively for cameras had risen in Rochester, and a vast plant for general photographic-supply manufacture was in existence on a plot of land in the little township of Greece, adjoining Rochester. Greece has long since become part of the larger city, but Kodak Park is still the dominant element in its economic landscape.

The full extent of Kodak expansionism was revealed in a new creation in 1901. At that time large corporations were making efforts to circumvent the eleven-year-old Sherman Antitrust Act, which, theoret-

ically at least, placed a barrier in the way of the mergers that were taking place at an accelerating rate. One acceptable device was the holding company, which owned the stock of various subsidiaries and managed them as one, though they remained technically independent "competitors." New Jersey's legal code smiled on holding companies, and so, in the same year that saw the creation of the world's first billion-dollar corporation, United States Steel, Eastman Kodak of New Jersey was likewise incorporated. Its capital was certainly more modest than U.S. Steel's, a mere thirty-five million, but it was no infant. The companies involved were Eastman Kodak of Rochester, the General Aristo Company of Rochester (an establishment manufacturing photographic paper and supplies), and Kodak, Ltd., of London—these three with factories in Rochester and Jamestown, New York, and Harrow, England; and in addition the Eastman Kodak Société Anonyme Française and the Kodak Gesellschaft, headquartered respectively in Paris and Berlin. All these operating firms had branch offices in New York, San Francisco, Liverpool, Glasgow, Brussels, Lyon, Milan, Vienna, Moscow, St. Petersburg, and Melbourne. By 1907 Eastman would be the boss of five thousand employees around the world. By 1915, during the first administration of Woodrow Wilson, he would also be under heavy attack from the United States government as a monopolistic superpower of photography, dominating more than 80 per cent of the market and forcing suppliers and dealers throughout the country to dance to his tune and accept his terms.

Kodak's response was to point out the existence of at least four other important camera manufacturers, eight makers of film, and a number of rivals in the supply business. But the fact was that none of them approached Eastman's giant company in scope, and finally Eastman was forced to avoid federal prosecution by authorizing an out-of-court settlement that divested his organization of several subsidiaries. The company remained large and diversified, however—sometimes to the bemusement of its founder, according to one story of post–World War I years. At that time the company went into a number of allied fields arising out of its chemical operations. These included the manufacture of cellulose, wood alcohol, and other ingredients and by-products of film. Among the spin-offs were synthetic fabrics, and when Eastman was shown some Celanese neckties made by his company in 1930, he mused aloud: "All I had in mind was to make enough money so that my mother would never have to work again."

This huge expansion rested, ultimately, on Eastman's ability to deliver what his advertisements promised in the dawning age of ballyhoo —a good camera, which, through the years, became more and more portable and inexpensive. In 1890 a folding model of the Kodak appeared, enabling some reduction in the size of the basic box. Further work yielded the Pocket Kodak in 1895, which was so instantaneously successful that within a short time after its announcement Eastman's European demand alone was for two thousand a month, and he was writing that he would "strain every nerve" to boost production to six hundred daily. In 1898 the Folding Pocket Kodak was introduced, only 1½ inches thick and 6½ inches long, producing a 2½-inch-by-3½-inch negative, which remained the standard size for years.

Like Henry Ford, Eastman was eager to get his product into the maximum number of hands. He preferred the profits of a mass rather than an elite market and therefore insisted on production economies and technical improvements that cut costs so that the price steadily sank from the twenty-five dollars asked for the original Kodak. The Bull's Eye model of 1896 (one of many variants of the basic camera in differing finishes and cases) cost twelve dollars, and a more modest type, the Falcon, was only five. In 1900 Eastman reached the apparent ultimate in price reduction, however, and also made a shrewd bid for a future generation of Kodak users, with the Brownie. This small box camera cost a single dollar. It took a six-exposure roll of film, purchasable for fifteen cents. It was advertised as something that could be "Operated by Any School Boy or Girl," and Eastman Kodak encouraged the youngsters to form Brownie Camera Clubs (blank constitutions, prepared in advance— like Eastman's bread mixes—were sent out on request) and to compete for prizes for the best pictures made with Brownies.

It is hard to know if any photographic careers were begun with Brownies, but there is the testimony of the distinguished pioneer Edward Steichen that he began with another Eastman Kodak model. It was a secondhand detective camera sold to him when he was sixteen, in 1895, and loaded in the darkroom by the dealer. Beginners may be cheered to note that when the fifty-exposure film was returned, only one shot was found printable.

Halfway through 1904 George Eastman celebrated his fiftieth birthday. It was a triumphant half-century mark. He was a mighty entrepreneur and a wealthy man. In the next year he demonstrated his affluence by moving into a new residence that was in effect an upstate New York palace. Its three stories contained thirty-seven rooms, twelve bathrooms, and nine fireplaces; it was surrounded by gardens and hot-houses, for Eastman loved flowers; and it had two organs, for he was likewise fond (though somewhat un-discriminatingly) of music. Its walls sported originals by Corot, Whistler, Rembrandt, and Titian, and its library had fine editions, mostly untouched, of Thackeray, Dickens, Hawthorne, Scott, Balzac, and Trollope. The installation of Eastman and his mother in their new estate was celebrated with a dinner party that spoke volumes about the Kodak King's style and taste. The guests were fed caviar, bouillon, halibut timbales with truffle sauce, breaded sweetbreads, tenderloin of beef with mushrooms, partridges with bread sauce, pumpkin pie, and nesselrode pudding, all washed down with vodka, Rhine wine, punch, and champagne. After this aristocratic banquet, a quartet sang *Boys of the Old Brigade, America, In the Good Old Summer Time, Marching Through Georgia, It's Always Fair Weather, Annie Laurie,* and *Teasing.* Then there were fireworks, topped off by what the handsomely printed and bound menu and program called "A Few Acts of Vaudeville."

Two years later Eastman's mother died, and he never took another woman into the house to be its mistress. Hundreds of guests occupied it, enjoyed the fresh flowers, and shared with their host his regular mealtime concerts by a private organist and his weekly evening musicales. Eastman also liked to invite the pretty young wives of his business associates and other friends to luncheons, at which he would cook for them, compliment them, josh them, shower them with small gifts—and scrupulously avoid any deep relationship with any of them. Though Rochester gossips were always ready with rumors of secret liaisons, Eastman lived in a house that always had about it something of the affectedness, the lack of human seasoning, of a wealthy and lonely bachelor's residence. He was a comforting and comfortable host, yet sometimes he seemed to be on display in his own home.

At the company's headquarters, his role changed. He remained the chief of a deliberately simplified organization, making the big decisions and constantly reviewing the figures that were forever being neatly columned for his eyes. But a huge array of managers, assistant managers, superintendents, assistant superintendents, foremen, and assistant foremen (375, all told, in 1908) kept operations running without his intervention in the day-to-day details that it had once been his challenge and pleasure to oversee. The research department plunged ever deeper into complex chemical problems beyond Eastman's theoretical grasp, though when results were achieved, they were presented to him to develop, to market, and to enfold in a kind of parental pride. He was far from a stranger to his own organization—but he was also no longer the man who, with Strong, Reichenbach, Walker, and others, had dirtied his own hands at drawing tables, fussed over emulsions, and experienced the elations and glooms. of those moments when a new idea is first tried.

Without a wife and children or an active, participating role in his company's work, Eastman needed other outlets for his energies, and he found them. He became a major benefactor of the city of Rochester, which he had given wealth and status beyond the dreams of even the most ambitious promoters. ("Wherever the photographic art is practiced," a local newspaper beamed in 1898, "there Rochester is known. . . . As the purchaser turns to Pittsburgh for steel . . . and to Chicago for grain, so does he turn to Rochester for photographic goods.") Eastman financed an orchestra, a theatre, a Municipal Bureau of Research, and a Chamber of Commerce building for his fellow townsmen and poured money into the modest University of Rochester, enabling it to add a distinguished medical school and a music con-

servatory and to upgrade itself dramatically in endowment. He also exerted a strong influence on Rochester's political life. Overtly, he put his support in the 1920's behind a conversion of the city's government to a city-manager format (a businessmen's and reformers' dream of efficient, nonpartisan rule). What other pressures he and Kodak exerted are still shadowed. It is enough to say, however, that one associate recalled, after Eastman's death, that he was the object of "near-hatred" to some Rochesterians who resented "the enormous control he exerted over his fellow citizens." The sound of civic applause may have drowned out the hisses, but they were there.

Rochester, however, was not the limit of his philanthropic outreach. He gave away nearly seventy-five million dollars before his death. A large share of that sum went to the Massachusetts Institute of Technology. (A modest as well as a generous giver, Eastman donated to M.I.T. for many years under the name "Mr. Smith.") There were also generous benefactions to two Negro colleges, Hampton and Tuskegee, and to dental clinics in various cities of the world—a pet project, for some per-

Eastman as the shadows gathered, in 1928
CULVER

sonal reason. Merely keeping track of the projects financed by his gifts could have become a totally absorbing occupation in itself. But Eastman also found time to play, after his fashion, as befitted the man who had taught the country to picture itself at play. He was an inveterate hunter, roaming the world at the head of large parties of friends and servants and bringing back from Africa and other exotic places packing cases laden with skins and heads for the walls of his home. Naturally, there were always copious photographic records of such safaris, made by the best and latest equipment.

He owned houses and lands; he owned a great corporation; in a sense, he was an important part-owner of the city of his rearing. Yet the report of everyone close to him was that he remained somewhat shy, content to ascribe his condition mostly to destiny, even slightly oppressed by a sense that he had a continuing responsibility to prove his usefulness to the world. He seemed to struggle against taking success or happiness for granted.

Sometime during 1931, when he was seventy-seven, Eastman began to suffer from a spinal ailment that threatened to make him a cripple. On March 14, 1932, he retired to an upstairs bedroom and, tidy to the end, neatly laid a folded towel over his chest and put a bullet through his heart. Beside him on a table was a note: "To my Friends: My work is done. Why wait?"

It was a lean, undemonstrative final farewell, in keeping with the style he had set himself. Perhaps the problem of his later life was that, in a sense, his work was already done by 1901, when the burdened but briskly moving days and nights of experiment and effort culminated in the great company that had created the camera that anyone—anyone at all—could buy, use, and enjoy. Perhaps the rest was only a comfortable twilight. ☆

Reginald Marsh

CONTINUED FROM PAGE 35

On one of my last visits to him I found him at work on a familiar subject, the Coney Island steeplechase. A British sailor and a girl are astride the wooden horse that races along a rail. The girl is blithe and smiling, as usual, but the sailor has died and the horse is like the horses in a medieval Triumph of Death. Its eyes are rolling, and its nostrils are distended.

"I can't finish it," Marsh said. "It's dead and I'm going to throw it away." He had taken a gray pigment and painted out the background, leaving sailor, girl, and horse isolated. "Don't throw it away," I said. "Give it to me." He handed it to me as if he were glad to be rid of it. I think that with this painting he had demolished the form which had sustained him. A change of title wouldn't serve now. *La Commédia è finita.*

Mr Laning, the well-known muralist, contributed to our pages "Memoirs of a WPA Painter" (October, 1970) and "Spoon River Revisited" (June, 1971). His recent book, The Act of Drawing, *was published by McGraw-Hill.*

The Grand Reconnaissance

CONTINUED FROM PAGE 48

do. In one of his few letters from the expedition Gunnison provided a vivid description of an officer's life on the New Mexican frontier:

It is amusing, surprizing and disgusting to hear the officers describe society in New Mexico. According to their *observation,* there's nothing like chastity regarded by man, woman, or priest. . . . Few girls are married until they have been seduced and have a child. . . . They arrive at puberty at eleven or twelve years and marry from eleven to fourteen. One beautiful woman was named who was a grand mother at 29 and though now appearing in the flower of her age, her grand daughter is ready to be married.

With its limited range, social life at Fort Massachusetts did not detain Gunnison's party for very long.

They rested their animals and overhauled their gear, while a detachment under Beckwith rode off southward for Taos to get another mountain man to guide them over the treacherous Cochetopa Pass and into the valley beyond. Fortunately they returned with Antoine Leroux, one of the real veterans of the southern Rocky Mountain fur trade. Leroux had guided Kearny west to California in 1847. In 1851 he had taken Lieutenant Lorenzo Sitgreaves' expedition into the Navaho country

of New Mexico and Arizona, below the Grand Canyon and the San Francisco Peaks to the Colorado River and on to California; on that trip a Yampais arrow had all but paralyzed him. For the past few months he had been staying in Taos with the other mountain trappers, assiduously attending fandangoes and all-night drinking bouts.

With Leroux to guide them the explorers were in good hands. During the last weeks of August they moved up the San Luis Valley, and by the end of the month they were approaching the Cochetopa Pass. Everywhere the grandeur and serenity of nature was impressive, and the party's routine responded to its invitation. Gunnison would scout ahead with Leroux while Beckwith would urge along the train. Kern would ride off to some nearby prominence to sketch the terrain while Schiel and Creuzfeldt would collect rocks and plants for shipment to the Smithsonian in Washington.

On September 2 they cut their way with axes and shovels over the crest of the Cochetopa, thereby crossing the Continental Divide. And during the next week, led by Leroux, they descended by stages into the valley of the present-day Gunnison River, which the captain himself

called the Grand. The only disturbing sign was an Indian smoke signal that arose against the sky beyond the mountains to the northwest in mistaken answer to a cook's runaway campfire. Then one day the advance party found itself suddenly surrounded by nearly two hundred Paiute Indians well mounted on captured Navaho ponies and arrogantly scowling at the white interlopers and demanding tribute. What had become a tense situation was shortly disposed of by Leroux. Speaking to the chief, he declared:

We have good weapons, much powder, and much lead. If you want to fight, so be it. We will fight with you and kill many of your warriors. The white father has many brave warriors. He will punish your transgressions. He has sent us to ride through your land and see what his red children are doing.

With that the red men became more hospitable and vanished shortly afterward. The explorers' route took them along the gorgeous high canyons of the Gunnison, across the barren divide west to the Uncompahgre, down that river to the Gunnison again, then over the Grand River (the main Colorado).

One day an entire Indian band appeared in a friendlier manner and, camping on a riverbank beside the caravan, hopefully awaited presents, shouting far into the night to their comrades on the other shore to swim across and join the party—and tell their friends about it, too. The hard-pressed Leroux found himself in the embarrassing position of having to spend the night sharing sleeping quarters with a native chief, one of whose fellow chiefs the scout had once killed in an altercation over a horse. But after much smoking and giving of presents the explorers eventually departed in peace.

From the Grand they made their way across a great barren artemisia plain covered with agate and other conglomerate rocks, relics of whole formations that, as Schiel pointed out, had almost vanished, "as it were, before our eyes." To the north were the colorful bands of the Book Cliffs. To the south, though none of the explorers noted it, were the fantastic eroded arches (now preserved as a national monument) that mark the entrance to the rugged country around the confluence of the Green and the Grand.

After passing the Green River the party made directly west up the broad sloping incline of the San Raphael Swell to the base of the Wasatch Mountains, which they could see dead ahead of them for several days. October 12 found them encamped near the entrance to Wasatch Pass, ready to cross over into the Great Basin. Captain Gunnison had thus far led his expedition successfully through some of the wildest and most difficult country in western North America, and they all had passed safely through the dangerous Ute country. Sometime after crossing the Grand River, Antoine Leroux had deemed them safe enough and himself turned back through Indian country for New Mexico and a rendezvous with Lieutenant Whipple and his thirty-fifth-parallel survey.

Meanwhile, as Gunnison's expedition was nearing its objective, Frémont's rival party, backed by eastern capitalists, was four months behind the Army topographers and following the same route. Because of his late start, however, Frémont found the Cochetopa Pass route considerably more difficult than had Gunnison. He followed the topographer's wagon ruts for a time, but deep snow soon obliterated the tracks, leaving the fate of the party up to the navigational skill of Frémont and his Delaware Indian guides. First the snow, then temperatures below 30 degrees, then starvation overtook them. It was 1848 all over again, and one night, somewhere near the Green River, Frémont made his men solemnly promise, no matter what the emergency, never to resort to cannibalism as had his previous company. Saved from despair and death only by Frémont's indomitable will, the party pushed on over the Wasatch Mountains to eventual safety at Parowan in southern Utah. One day short of safety, however, Oliver Fuller, the assistant topographer, quietly died of exposure and the effects of having frozen his legs and feet from the knees down. Solomon Carvalho, the photographer, a city man at heart, and F. W. von Egloffstein, the topographical artist, a portly gentleman who wasn't much used to starvation, had had enough, and on March 1, 1854, they arrived in Salt Lake City clad in rags, still hungry, and eager for civilized companionship. The Pathfinder's luck was down. Once again a Frémont expedition had ended ingloriously, if not tragically.

Gunnison, on the other hand, four months ahead on the trail and oblivious to Frémont's difficulties, was nearing the end of his labors, and he spent a week passing over the Wasatch Mountains in a painstaking approach to the valley of the Sevier River. Once across the mountains the party was in Mormon country

and what could practically be considered civilization. However, when they visited Manti, near the great bend of the Sevier River, and found the entire population barricaded in their houses, fearful of an Indian attack, Gunnison learned of potential dangers from savages in the valley of the Great Salt Lake. From Manti he wrote to his wife:

There is a war between the Mormons and the Indians and parties of less than a dozen do not dare to travel. We did not know what a risk we have lately been running until coming here for I have been riding carelessly in the mountains hunting roads ahead and other curious capers. . . .

It was to be his last letter.

Upon his return to camp near Fillmore, Utah, Gunnison had reason to congratulate himself. He had located a new military road from Taos most of the way to the Great Salt Lake. He had laid out a new route for westbound emigrants that would enable them to start later in the season. He had plotted a military trail that led right into the heart of the Mormon stronghold. And finally, he had convincingly shown that the Cochetopa Pass route, while passable, was clearly inferior to the Stansbury route via the Medicine Bow River and the Laramie Plains farther to the north in present-day Wyoming —Senator Benton, John C. Frémont, and Edward Fitzgerald Beale notwithstanding. But tasks remained, among them the exploration of the lower Sevier River for a suitable railroad crossing. Somehow he secured the services of two Mormon brothers, G. G. and William Potter, who consented to act as guides in an effort to find the best railroad pass over the mountains and down into the Great Basin.

Now on October 25, Gunnison, Kern, Creuzfeldt, Bellows, the Mormon William Potter, and a corporal's guard of seven men from the escort left the main party encamped on the upper river and headed downstream toward Sevier Lake. Lieutenant Beckwith was left in charge of the main camp. At eleven the following morning a scouting party he had just sent out of camp returned with a tattered and bloody dragoon from Gunnison's party who was so weak and exhausted that he was barely able to talk. He was the corporal in charge of the escort, and between gasps for breath he sobbed out his story. Less than five hours ago, just at dawn, Captain Gunnison and all his men had been massacred by an overwhelming force of Indians hidden along the Sevier River. As far as he knew, he alone had survived.

As it turned out, four men had survived. But the other accounts added little to the corporal's. After leaving the main camp Captain Gunnison's command had spent most of the twenty-fifth of October moving slowly down the valley. They had marched about eleven miles before making camp on the edge of the river near a willow grove. The arduous marches of the previous months were behind them, and officers and men alike refused to take the daily Indian signal fires seriously. Some of the party went out hunting along the river just before nightfall. And then they all retired after a good campfire meal. The next morning, just as they had begun to stir themselves, all hell broke loose. Shrieks and yells, showers of arrows, reports of guns, men screaming in terror, horses neighing wildly and breaking their picket ropes in a dash for freedom—it was an Indian attack, or was it the Mormons? In any case it was doubtless every man for himself, with the losers left on the battlefield.

The rest of the story belongs to the attackers, young braves from Chief Kenosh's band of Sevier River Paiutes. On the afternoon of the twenty-fifth several young Paiute Indians were out hunting ducks when they heard the firing of the soldiers

in the marshes along the river. Incensed at all white men for the recent murder of one of their chiefs, they followed the hunters back to camp, observed it, and then hurried to their own village, where, in a wild dance, they whipped up a war party to ambush the soldiers. About midnight they departed. There were about a score in all—Mishoquop, Sam, Pants, Tomwants, Jimmy Knights, Toady, Doctor Jacob, Nunkiboolits, Shipoke—their names absurdly incongruous with the mission they were set on performing.

When they reached the campsite, Mishoquop deployed his forces professionally. One group hid in the willows along the river to the south of the camp, others to the east. The rest stationed themselves behind a ridge to the north and somewhat back from the river. All three sides were covered in crossfire, and the river itself on the west offered little chance for escape. Then they waited.

At dawn the cook arose, raked up the fire, and began his breakfast chores. Professor Creuzfeldt stood, hands outstretched, warming himself by the fire. One by one the men began to stir. It was rapidly getting light. Captain Gunnison, who had left his tent to go to wash, had just moved past the door of his tent into the center of the camp when Mishoquop gave the signal to fire. At the first barrage the soldiers panicked. They ran in all directions, some without trousers, some without tunics, most without any thought of guns or resistance. The coolest ran for the horses, the rest just anywhere away from the enemy. One dragoon managed to mount his horse and start out of camp. At the flash of a gun his horse reared, and at the same instant the dragoon fell pierced with arrows. Another soldier vaulted onto the horse from a dead run and dashed away to safety. Whooping and howling as loudly in fright as the Indians did in triumph, the soldiers were shot down as they ran or

rode away from camp right into the Indians concealed behind the ridge to the north. Creuzfeldt and Kern fell by the fire. With the first barrage Gunnison rushed forward to rally his command. He too went down, riddled with arrows. In all, three men died at the riverside and six on the plains beside the willow grove. Four managed to escape: two on horseback, one by hiding in the bushes after his horse threw him, and the fourth by swimming the river. In a few minutes it was all over, and the savages, full of triumphant revenge, swarmed onto the field to mutilate the dead explorers.

It was the only great disaster of the Pacific Railroad Surveys and would have a strong impact upon the people of the day. The leadership of the exploring party devolved upon Lieutenant Beckwith, who led what was left of the command on a sad march north to Salt Lake City and comparative civilization.

After a winter of recuperation at Salt Lake City, Beckwith's party took to the field again in an effort to complete the task assigned to their thirty-eighth-parallel survey. In the early spring, even before the snows had melted, they explored eastward, searching for suitable railroad passes across the Wasatch Mountains and into the valley of the Green River, where Beckwith hoped to link up with Stansbury's route of 1850. By April 22 he and his men had completed their task, and a practicable central railroad route had been located from the Platte River as far west as the Mormon capital.

Upon receiving authorization from Washington, Beckwith determined to finish the central survey all the way across the Great Basin to California. On May 5, 1854, he led his surveyors out across the Basin, where for days they threaded their way through mountain passes and over the arid and dusty valleys of what had once been a primeval lake bed, seeing no one except a few wretched Digger Indians who lived on rats and crickets and slept in crude stick huts called wickiups. When at last the surveyors reached the Sierra Nevada, on the far side of the Basin, they searched out a new railroad pass (Madelin Pass) and crossed over into California, linking the valley of the Mississippi with the Sacramento Valley on a great central route that ran north of the one that Senator Benton had proposed. In the light of their own hard-won experience, however, it was one that appeared to be far more useful. It offered few mountain obstacles. And it could take advantage of the already existing Mormon settlements for labor in constructing the road as well as for a ready-made market for some of the products that the road would carry.

The results of all the Pacific Survey expeditions had indeed been startling. Every commander of a field party—Stevens, Parke, Pope, Whipple, and Beckwith—reported the discovery of "the most practicable and economical railroad route to the Pacific Ocean." The tired Congress was right back where it had started. But for Davis there was no doubt: the southern route along the thirty-second parallel was the best. It mattered little that Beckwith and the weary men of the Gunnison expedi-

tion had discovered what was perhaps a superior line or that the equally intrepid Whipple had led his expedition upon what was plainly another practical line along the thirty-fifth parallel. Davis was sure he saw things more clearly than most people, and his subordinates in the topographical bureau backed him up. It was the southern course or none.

Congress would not agree, and the choice for now was none. No section, North, South, or West, could agree on a route, and no through railroad was completed until 1869, when the Golden Spike went down at Promontory, Utah. By then the victorious North had control of Congress and could put through lines wherever it chose.

The Pacific Railroad Surveys were, for a time, a seeming failure, but only for political reasons. Eventually, however, rails covered nearly all the routes, and run to this day. Meanwhile, the explorers had produced a monumental inventory of our unsettled empire beyond the Mississippi. Lieutenant G. K. Warren's overall survey map of 1857 was a landmark in American cartography. Jules Marcou and William Blake produced the first comprehensive geologic maps of the West, though the second man, Blake, sharply criticized the work of the first, behavior not unprecedented in

the scholarly world. Back in Washington, Spencer F. Baird of the Smithsonian Institution supervised a team of zoologists who published massive volumes on the birds, mammals, reptiles, and fishes of the West. Each of the surveys had a report on geology and botany. Two reports even included discussions of Indian ethnology. With their stilted formalities, the big, weighty volumes are still fascinating to read and pore over, illuminated by dramatic landscapes and splendid maps and offering the flash of humor and the thrill of danger and discovery.

Thus the West was first widely mapped, classified, catalogued, painted, described, and published for everyone to see. The price was a bargain. In the long run science and the generations to come were the ultimate beneficiaries, and Gunnison's name, like that of the other great Pacific Railroad explorers, lives on, appropriately affixed to those wonders of nature that he helped to discover and that he hoped to conquer for civilization.

William H. Goetzmann is professor of history and director of the American Studies Program at the University of Texas. His book, Exploration and Empire, *won a Pulitzer Prize in 1967, and he is currently working on a study of American intellectual history.*

A Dearth of Heroes

CONTINUED FROM PAGE 7

all, too likely to prove attainable, at least in some measure. Perhaps we dimly realize, in some deeply significant way, that, as Bertrand Russell says, the essence of the ideal is to be *not* real. Perhaps there is in us a forgotten, secret, starved yearning for a poetry of grandeur, for the freedom of selflessness, for the exaltation of vision. And so we have Washington and Jefferson.

Indeed, in a world where Franklin as hero seems what you yourself, with just a little luck, might be, Washington is clearly what you know you could never be. He is, after all, something beyond the range of daydreams. He beckons, but from a great distance, like a snow-covered peak in sunlight.

Washington was, as Wecter says, "glacial." In peaceful times he could

lay off from his farming to go deer hunting, was a devoted rider to hounds, acted in amateur theatricals, loved to dance for hours at a stretch, and was not above taking his ease and eating watermelon on the front porch of his farmhouse, known as Mount Vernon. But nobody ever regarded him as folksy or ever dared to slap him on the back or dared, more than once, to lay hand to his sleeve.

He stood, also, at the distance of great wealth, holding, as John Adams put it in praising him for leaving luxury for a hazardous struggle, one of the "first fortunes upon the continent." It was a fortune which, in addition to that acquired by marriage, he had accumulated in ways very different from Franklin's and dispensed in a way even more different —that of the great squire and not the burgher. As a commander he never courted favor but was a stern disciplinarian, fair but tough; once he erected a gallows forty feet high and used it. Even his self-command was, somehow, unhuman in its reach. And he lacked all arts of the orator. Unlike Franklin, who was a master of the art of persuasion, supposedly so fundamental to power in a democracy, Washington never lifted a finger or opened a lip to persuade anybody.

Yet this man became the prime hero of a raw democracy. Somehow, from early manhood, an air of destiny hung about him, and after the first bullets had whizzed harmlessly past him ("I heard the bullets whistle," he said, "and believe me, there is something charming in the sound"), he seems to have believed in his destiny. Destiny aside, what he did have to show the world was a massive self-certainty, studiously modelled on that of the Roman stoics, a cold serenity in the face of defeat, the impression of power in reserve, fixity of purpose, and devotion to principle (which meant, in the end, devotion to "liberty"), with selfish concern and ambition absorbed into the concept of duty. When the time came to lay aside command, he could do it as casually as though taking off an old coat.

If Franklin was a hero who sometimes seemed to be created in the image of a gifted Polonius, with a dash of Sam Slick added, Washington was a hero created in something close to the image of God. Franklin might tell you how to live and get

rich. Washington might, if need arose, teach you how to die. As for Jefferson, he—who had never heard even one bullet whistle past his ears —could teach you neither how to live nor how to die; but he could teach you how to envision a world worth living in or dying for.

We may say that these three are the prime American heroes, each summing up in relatively pure form one of the ideals that, in varying combinations and with varying modifications, have persisted in American life. The ideals appear, sometimes, in very peculiar combinations and modifications. For instance, to twist the Bible story, if Emerson spoke with the voice of Jacob his visionary prophecy of America, his hands were the hands of Esau—that is, not of Jefferson, but of Franklin, that archetypal exponent of "self-reliance," who might well have said what Emerson did say, that "money . . . smells as sweet as roses." And if Grant, from 1861 to 1865, showed something of the massive self-certainty and fixity of purpose of a Washington, he showed later, in a painfully debased form, some of the less endearing traits of Poor Richard.

In tracing the mutations of the species *heros Americanus*, Wecter is inevitably concerned with defining the essential qualities. But what the hero cannot be looms as significantly as what he must be.

First, there are by American standards certain professions and occupations that are unheroic—or at least have never furnished us a hero. No artist, writer, scholar, philosopher, physician, or saint need apply for a pedestal. He may be a very worthy fellow, but in our society no man from the groups we have named is the stuff from which heroes are made. And here, with surprise, we must note that a scientist need not apply, either. Even if our advertisements celebrate the man in white holding up the test tube, it is science,

not the scientist, that we revere, and what we revere about science is, in the end, its practical benefits. Certainly, our only "scientific" heroes, Franklin and Edison, do nothing to contradict this view.

The life of the mind and spirit are not for us—or, at least on the record, are not for our hero-makers. In Europe even minor writers and artists get streets named for them, in provincial towns as well as great cities, and get statues in parks and commemorative plaques on buildings associated with their careers. Even foreigners may get such notice; in Sicily, for instance, at Taormina, a farmhouse bears a marble plaque proclaiming that D. K. [*sic*] Lawrence once lived there. In America, nothing. Perhaps a rare high school or library, and that is it. Literature, philosophy, science, the arts (including the art of healing)—these things, perhaps all right in their places, are adjuncts to our civilization as most of our citizens conceive it: frills for women and eggheads.

Among those things that an American hero cannot be, at the other end of the spectrum from the life of the mind or spirit, is the "strong man par excellence," neither as political leader nor military victor. We have no Stalins or Napoleons among our heroes. We admire strength, even ferocious strength, as in Jackson, and we have made a number of generals into Presidents, but the generals that really carry the aura of the heroic had some overplus beyond generalship. One cannot imagine the pure military man, General Patton, for instance, in the White House, no matter what his professional genius. If Grant became President, we must remember that he was, in one sense, a most unsoldierly soldier, unlike Sherman, with no military tone and with a humanizing personal story of failure.

In fact, somewhat surprisingly and hearteningly, failure does not disqualify a man from being an American hero. But he must be a dead-game failure; he must be able to convert practical defeat into a victory of spirit. The Western badman, dead with a gun hot in each hand and all his wounds in front, touches us in the old primitive way; or Davy Crockett on the walls of the Alamo, or Jim Bowie of the famous knife, in the Alamo, too, having the cot on which he lay sick carried across the line scratched by a sword point in the packed earth of the courtyard to join those who would die rather than surrender. Lee, of course, is our best example of the failure as hero. In failure he became even more of a hero in the South than he had been in the days when he carried the fortunes of the Confederacy across his saddlebows; but his transcendent triumph was to become, in spite of the curse pronounced on him by that Northern almost-hero, the almost-martyr Senator Charles Sumner ("I hand him over to the avenging pen of history"), a hero in the North, too, with none less than Charles Francis Adams, the younger, who had once commanded black troops in blue uniforms, to officiate at the ceremonies of canonization. But long since, Lee had won a final and inexpungible victory over Grant by setting his dignity in defeat as a contrast to the corruption and vulgarity in which the victor Grant was basking in the White House.

In success or failure, in elective office or not, first of all the hero must be, as Wecter says, the "people's choice." To be a hero at all he must command, in one way or another, their imagination and acceptance. To do this he must, in one way or another, be a figure of power, even a father figure; but in spite of power he must keep his personal modesty. Somehow, even the glacial dignity of Washington was made acceptable by his unselfish care for his men and his calm willingness to return, like Cincinnatus, to the plow. He was, after all, a farmer and a good one, and the proud possessor of a silver cup awarded by an agricultural society as "a premium for raising the largest jackass."

There are, indeed, all sorts of paradoxicalities in our requirements for the heroic role. The hero, as we have said, must be strong, though never a "strong man." He must be willing to lead, but a claim to infallibility, even to those who cry out for the father figure, is offensive. In a time of great crisis, there is always the demand for immediate and decisive action and for total solution, but history shows that our greatest heroes have given the impression not so much of putting into effect a preconceived and infallible program of total solution, but of working something out, painfully and with not infrequent setbacks. The military careers of both Washington and Grant, for instance, had something of the air of self-education conducted in public. The notion that Lincoln was a repository of divine wisdom would have appalled the critics of his war policies or the abolitionists. It was a notion that took root in the popular mind only after he was safely tucked away—victorious and dead. Franklin Delano Roosevelt knew the art of combining long-range confidence ("The only thing we have to fear is fear itself") with a willingness to accept the method of trial and error. And he could politically afford error because of two things: he could convince the electorate of the steadfastness of his principles and the worth of his objectives and could, while trying to realize those objectives, give the electorate, by the potent device of the Fireside Chat, the impression that the process of trial and error was one in which they, somehow, were significantly participating.

Our hero must, as we have said, give the impression of power without any claim to infallibility and must wear power with humility. But the humility, too, must be of a special order: it must be associated with power, but the power must appear as an instrument of the common good. There is something of a contradiction implicit here. The power must, on the one hand, be *really* the hero's—otherwise he would not be a hero; but, on the other, he must not admit to being more than an instrument. Logically, this would land us in the notion that the hero is a force making history, creating events, and at the same time a mere by-product of history; but the folk mind—or, in the end, any individual mind—can entertain simultaneously both propositions, each one representing a profound and compelling need. That is enough, and logic be damned. The contradiction, indeed, is absorbed into experience and restated: the hero must be powerful enough to protect his people, but the power thus exercised is depersonalized and becomes a creation, as it were, of the need and the will of the people. This is the mystery of democracy.

The mystery is even more potent when the hero dies for his people —his death being the ritual by which the man is totally absorbed into the role. As a matter of fact, though our hero is often hailed in the flesh, we may paraphrase for him what was once said of the Indian: the only really good hero is a dead one. The hero dead is safe, more or less, from envy and detraction, and if while living he had the heroic virtues, the distance of death, removing small blemishes and complicating factors, works to stylize the virtues, to give them a hieratic simplicity. These somewhat negative values of death are transmuted into overwhelmingly positive ones when the death has the aura of sacrifice. Lincoln is, of course, the perfect example, but the cases of Garfield and McKinley are more instructive; for, as is generally agreed, neither had much claim to the heroic role beyond a talent for getting in the way of a bullet. As for John F.

Kennedy, time has not yet fixed his place on the scale of our martyred Presidents; we do not know what slot he will occupy in the considerable space between Lincoln at the top and Garfield and McKinley competing for the bottom. In the end he may well be closer to those heroes-by-accident than to the Olympian Father Abraham. At least in the case of Kennedy (and that of his brother), the martyrdom saved him from the need to face up, with money on the card, to the major crises in which he was involved, and the aura of heroism he carried depended more on expectations for the future than on the hard facts of the past.

But in reference to our general question, the assassin's bullet is not specifically required for martyrdom. Undoubtedly, the fact that Franklin Delano Roosevelt died in office, ironically at the moment when victory loomed near, gave something of an impression of martyrdom; and it may help to consolidate his claims to heroic stature. He died in the line of duty, with his boots on, for his country. For his country—and that, it would seem, is the prime requirement, whether the hero is statesman, warrior, explorer, inventor, or whatnot. The hero must "serve" his people.

Even if, as Wecter has argued, there is a characteristic profile for the American hero, there are still fashions in heroism. In one of W. D. Howells' least-read books, *A Traveler from Altruria*, a satirical fiction in which the visitor from a decent and rational society (safely mythical, of course) tries to make sense of America, one of our citizens (as of the year 1900) explains to him the shifts in fashion, after the Civil War, of the "ideal of greatness":

. . . I should say that within a generation our ideal had changed twice. Before the war [the Civil War], and during all the time from the revolution onward, it was undoubtedly the great politician, the publicist, the statesman. As we grew older and began to have an intellectual life of our own, I think the literary fellows had a pretty good share of the honors that were going; that is, such a man as Longfellow was popularly considered a type of greatness. When the war came, it brought the soldier to the front, and there was a period of ten or fifteen years when he dominated the national imagination. That period passed, and the great era of material prosperity set in. The big fortunes began to tower up, and heroes of another sort began to appeal to our admiration. I don't think there is any doubt but the millionaire is now the American ideal. . . .

In a similar way Wecter analyzes the shifts of "taste and spirit in hero worship." By his version of events, there was, first, the "Silver Age" of our patriotism, the age of oratory and grandiosity, in which one "could hardly see the hero for the incense." Then from 1840 to the Civil War—to be resumed afterward and continued to about 1914—came the Age of Sentiment, in which the tender side of the lives of the great—love of mother, devotion to wives, children, and dumb beasts, and pity and other humane impulses—became the stock in trade; this was the period when one "could not see the hero for the tears." The Civil War demanded sterner stuff for the role of the hero, producing as its most awesome specimens the gigantic Lincoln, the noble Lee, and the grimly competent Grant; but the subsequent period—the period of the Great Barbecue—though it did, as Howells says, affirm a national ideal of the businessman, produced no hero who, by common consent, embodied that ideal. There was, in fact, a teeming host of pedestal-claimants, from Jay Gould through Jim Fisk and Commodore Vanderbilt on to Andrew Carnegie, but they seem to have killed off each other in the popular imagination. What emerged was a pair of heroes who, indeed, got rich, but whose success was not based on mere financial manipulation and organization; Ford and Edison had another kind of know-how, they could "make" something, electric light bulbs or tin lizzies—and this difference must reflect some credit on America, after all. In a backhand way, the canonization of Teddy Roosevelt bears some relation, too, to the popular attitude toward the world of business: if the heroic statue that might be erected to Teddy would properly have the right foot on San Juan Hill and the right hand lifting a sword in a gesture of command, it would have the left foot on the neck of a dragon labeled "the Trusts" and the left hand clutching a copy of the Supreme Court decision in the Northern Securities case.

World War I gave us Woodrow Wilson and certain military aspirants for the American pantheon, but, as Wecter observes, this was the only war that put no general in the White House and that has for its characteristic hero a nameless man. But in a deep ambiguity, the heroic role of the Unknown Soldier pointed not only, we may hazard, to the idea of the heroic in the common, but also to a contempt for heroism that was to characterize the age of the Great Boom. For that was also the Age of the Great Debunking, in which all heroes would be unmasked, usually by parlor Freudians, and the United States would be regarded as Just Another Sucker for having been conned into a crusade to Make the World Safe for Democracy.

Upon this cynicism and sophistication burst Lindbergh, with all the simplicities and ardors of the old American legend—the All-American Boy from the Heartland of America, a small-town boy, not bookish but very smart about gadgets, awkwardly good-looking, with rumpled blond hair, but without vanity, wearing a rumpled old blue suit. And he loved his mother; the first thing he did on arriving in Paris was to get a wire off to her. But Lindbergh did not usher in a new fashion. He was, in a sense, merely the last flickering gleam of an old one. The Big Media, then just getting the hang of things, took the hint and inflated the old fashion into a new that was a monstrous parody of the old.

The waning of Lindbergh's popularity merged with the atmosphere of the Depression. New and very un-American heroes were now being adopted; in some quarters Lenin, in others Trotsky; but in quarters more parochial there was the Common Man—a type figure with even deeper ambiguities than the Unknown Soldier. Sometimes—ideally considered—the image of the Common Man was taken as a celebration of the yearning for the excellent, for the heroic, in which all men may participate—and of the quality sung by Whitman in "the numberless unknown heroes equal to the greatest heroes known." But more frequently that image was taken as a celebration of (and as an alibi for) the merely average, with "commonness" taken to justify any lack of striving or aspiration, that is, with the Common Man as the image of the Anti-Hero writ large.

As Wecter has wittily pointed out, the "collective ideal of the little man" was in other countries making possible the new order of hero, represented by Mussolini, Hitler, and Stalin, the hero who was photographed "blessing peasant children" or, stripped to the waist, helping to "get the crops in"—the "triumphant sublimation of a million inferiority complexes" redeemed in the form of world-shaking power. In America, however, we never got that far, and the image of the Common Man remained faceless and abstract. The image had here, too, a sort of counterpoise: the faceless image prospered alongside a most readily identifiable and most uncommon man and hero-in-the-making, F.D.R. And here Wecter finishes his book with Pearl Harbor yet to come.

And with our own age yet to come.

Inevitably, we ask ourselves what Wecter, had he lived (he died in 1950, at the age of forty-four), would have made of the years since World War II—and what we may make of them. For whatever value literature may have as an index to life, our novels tell us that we live in the age of the Anti-Hero—or at least of the Slob-as-Hero. Certainly, in real life in America, we find God's plenty of slobs in leading roles, but the Slob-as-Hero may not be, after all, the type most characteristic of our time. With a poet's prescience, Ezra Pound, some fifty years ago, in "Mauberley" demanded:

> *What god, man, or hero*
> *Shall I place a tin wreath upon?*

Ours is the age of the Tin Wreath —no, of the Tin Hero, stamped out by the stamping mill of the media, to the order of the public relations man, with guaranteed built-in obsolescence. To put it another way, in an age of blab, of mass blankness, spurious literacy, prefabricated opinions, and predigested ideals that come out like a ribbon and lie flat on the brush, the celebrity, as Daniel J. Boorstin has put it in *The Image*, has long since taken the place of the hero. The hero is known for having done something; the celebrity is known for being known. The deed is the mark of the hero, mention in the gossip column that of the celebrity. In fact, the gossip column is both the womb and the Valhalla of the celebrity—but a Valhalla as crowded as a subway station at the rush hour; the great revolving door toward which the throngs push is marked "Eternity," but admits the celebrity, suddenly and irrevocably, and no doubt to his great surprise, into darkness.

"Time hath, my lord," says the wily Ulysses to the sulky Achilles in Shakespeare's *Troilus and Cressida*, "a wallet at his back," and in that wallet he puts "alms for oblivion." Even true fame, that is, may fade, but prefabricated fame doesn't even have a chance to fade. The essence of news is to be new, and the fame of the celebrity in its newest gloss lasts only until the next newscast: if it isn't in its newest gloss it will not be on the newscast. Celebrity is, paradoxically and pathetically, the death warrant of *the* celebrity. And pathetically we have seen a candidate for President —and a candidate, in the minds of many, for the status of hero—feel the need to attach himself to show-biz celebrities, presumably hoping that some of that glamour might rub off on him. And more recently, a P.R. expert who had a hand in the "selling" of another President to the country has divulged the arts whereby the vendible commodity was fabricated.

Have we, in America, had a hero in our time—that is, since World War II? I can think of only one man with a serious claim, Martin Luther King. The theme was high, the occasion noble, the stage open to the world's eye, the courage clear and against odds. And martyrdom came to purge all dross away. King seems made for the folk consciousness, and the folk consciousness is the Valhalla of the true hero—not the gossip column. King may even, someday, enter into the folk consciousness of the white world, which may yet underlie, at what depth it is hard to guess, the Culture of Blab. ☆

Martin Luther King

99

The Radio Priest CONTINUED FROM PAGE 41

The Radio League grew out of the letters I received in the early days, and I said, well, these people want to support me, and it costs a lot of money. Hundreds of thousands, millions of dollars eventually. As the program expanded to other stations, they began charging me regular commercial rates, which was right.

Your first direct involvement in domestic politics occurred in October, 1931, when you denounced the Depression policies of the Hoover administration—is that correct?

That's right, I had come to realize, and I was dismayed by this knowledge, that according to the laws of the United States at that time, the government was empowered to spend thousands of dollars on the pigs in Alabama and Georgia but not one cent for the relief of the people of those states. I tried to tell that to my congregation, and I used to say to them, how terribly unkind the American people are and how unskilled they are in the practical knowledge of running a country. I told them it was unfair to blame Mr. Hoover; after all, I used to say, he's *only* the Executive. Let me say this about Mr. Hoover. There never was a finer, more stalwart American gentleman than he was. He was also one of the best-educated Presidents we've ever had, with the possible exception of Woodrow Wilson, who had the education but lacked the judgment of Mr. Hoover. Well, President Hoover was probably the most harnessed Executive we've ever had, at a time when we needed one with more elasticity in his actions. Later on, years later, when he was living in New York at the Waldorf-Astoria, I went over to tender my heartfelt sympathies and apologies for anything I might have said while he was President, and he said, "Young man, I don't blame you. I was the symbol of our nation, and the nation needed castigation. As you know now, it wasn't my fault, but I would have been a cad"—that is the word he used—"if I had said, don't blame me, blame Congress." That was quite a heroic statement.

Then, early in 1932, you became an enthusiastic supporter of New York's Governor Franklin D. Roosevelt for President.

I liked Mr. Roosevelt, and I think he liked me, up to a point. He was the governor, and we had a mutual friend, Jimmy Walker, who was mayor of New York City. Jimmy had a flair for appointing competent people, who loved money, to the management of the city's affairs. Well, the investigation of the Walker administration by Judge [Samuel] Seabury was becoming embarrassing to Mr. Roosevelt, so one day the governor said to me, "You're

on the air. I wouldn't mind a little bit of help, to tell the truth." I reminded him that Jimmy was a friend, and he said, "Hell, he's friends with everybody. He's friends with you, he's friends with the pope, he's friends with Antichrist."

Did you consider yourself an active Roosevelt supporter?

I would say that my "impromptu" speech at the 1932 Democratic convention in Chicago swung a lot of votes to his candidacy. In fact, I think I was the last speaker before the nominations began. It was supposed to be extemporaneous and all that. "Hi there, Father. Why don't you come on up to the microphone and say a few words," but it was all, you know, carefully staged.

And Governor Roosevelt asked for your help in the Walker case?

He made it clear to me that he had to get rid of James, one way or the other. Seabury had finally submitted the charges against Walker to the governor, and Mr. Roosevelt had announced that he was going to give the mayor a personal hearing, so he invited me to come to Albany and sit in. The governor was concerned about the reaction of Catholic voters to his handling of the Walker case. So I sat in on the Albany hearing. It was a masterful performance by the governor, during which Mayor Walker embarrassed himself right out of office, and after it was over I came out, and Mr. Roosevelt was gesticulating to me, and I was smiling back, and the reporters could see that I was on his side.

And afterward Mayor Walker resigned and left the country. But before the Albany hearing you had said at a Communion breakfast in New York that the charges against Walker were part of a Communist plot to undermine respect for government. Were you shocked when these charges turned out to be true?

I said the accusations were too preposterous to believe. When they turned out to be true, I was shocked to death. I think most Americans were.

President Roosevelt appointed your friend Mayor Frank Murphy, of Detroit, to the governor-generalship of the Philippines. Some people have claimed that the appointment was a direct result of your support, while others, including Mrs. Roosevelt and Postmaster General James A. Farley, have denied it. What did happen?

I saw Mr. Roosevelt after he won the nomination, and he told me that he was very grateful for what I had done. "Padre," he said—he always called me Padre—"you can have any damned thing you want after this election." I said that there's not much I want, I can't take much; but, I said, I want to tell you a little bit of history that you might not know. I said that South America was supposed to be a Catholic continent. Whether or not they were good or bad Catholics, they did go under the flag of Catholicity. And I told Mr. Roosevelt that it was a curious phenomenon that all the European nations were represented by Catholic ambassadors but not the United States. You know, I told him, that they call us "*yanquis*" down there, even in Mexico; and the word didn't translate as "Yankee." It had come to mean, in political slang, high Freemasons. So I said to him, listen, get smart, because the day will come when we're going to need hemispheric solidarity—I was for that even then—so why don't you send a Catholic ambassador down there. And he said, "Hell, I never thought of that. It's a good idea." And he asked me to get him a list of qualified Catholics. I got a list together, and in December, after he had been elected, I went over to New York to see him. "Padre," he said, "terrible disappointment. I can't go through with that." I asked him why, and he told me that he had promised to make Cordell Hull the new Secretary of State, and Hull had already told certain people that they were going to be ambassadors down there. But, said Mr. Roosevelt, you can have anything else you want. So I said, what about the Philippines, and I suggested Frank Murphy, who had served my first Mass back in 1916 and had a lot on the ball. "You got it," he said, "he's it."

Who introduced you to Roosevelt?

That's a hard thing to say. I can't remember the time, from the time he was governor of New York, that I didn't know him. Later on my good friend Joe Kennedy, the father of the President, had me get very close to Mr. Roosevelt. That was before the President made Joe the chairman of the Securities and Exchange Commission.

The recurring theme of your broadcasts during this period was monetary reform. You charged that the Depression was a result of trying to maintain an impractical gold standard and insisted that the United States had a choice, as you put it, between revaluation and Christianity or repudiation and Bolshevism. How does your position appear in retrospect?

I wanted silver remonetized, of course, because I knew that there wasn't enough gold to go around. You see, there just isn't enough precious metal in the world to make it the basis of real wealth. If you study the history of money, as I have, and it goes back four thousand years before Christ, when all they had was gold and silver, you come to realize how international finance has been monopolized over the centuries by a small group of men who have had the power to manipulate the internal affairs of nations.

You spent a lot of radio time lecturing your audience on currency, didn't you?

When I went to a junior school in Canada, about the equivalent of the eighth grade here, we were taught money. In fact, it was taught along with geography. I remember how the teacher used to give each of us the name of a ship, and we had to take that ship from the port of Montreal all the way to Hong Kong, and we had to learn why the price of the Canadian dollar was different in all the various ports of the world—and why that price fluctuated from day to day. Well, economic geography just isn't taught in this country, and Americans just don't know a thing about money, and it's a hopeless situation trying to teach them anything, because we have the best dollar, so they still think—although it's off twenty-one cents today in Zurich.

You still keep in touch, don't you?

I'm sort of a bug on that situation, and I like to keep right abreast of that. One of the first things I get, at 4:30 A.M. every day, is the market price of the dollar in Switzerland.

When Al Smith announced that he was "for gold dollars as against baloney dollars," you accused him, on your broadcast of November 26, 1933, of being a paid stooge of the banking interests. What prompted you to attack the most prominent Catholic politician in the nation?

Mr. Roosevelt.

Would you say that historians have generally underestimated the strength, the closeness of your relationship with F. D. R.?

He wasn't the greatest President we've ever had. I knew it, and so did many of his associates. But I *liked* the man. People say I hated him, but I never did. I loved the man. When he was away from that darned desk of his and that long cigarette thing and sitting down with some of us or playing cards, there was no more gracious person that ever lived. You know, even then I wouldn't let anyone else attack Mr. Roosevelt, and I still won't. Isn't that funny? He wasn't a malicious man, either, don't ever think that. I don't think there was a bit of malice in the man's make-up. But I think he was unfortunate in the choice of some of his associates. A lot of them were square pegs, and I told him one time, I'll bet you wouldn't invite some of them down here for dinner.

In the middle of your campaign to have silver remonetized—I believe it was in April, 1934—Secretary of the Treasury Henry Morgenthau released, ostensibly with the President's approval, a list of persons and organizations with substantial investments in silver. Prominent on the list, with five hundred thousand ounces, was your Radio League. Who do you think was really responsible for this action?

I blame Morgenthau.

But surely Roosevelt knew about it?

I wouldn't say that. Many things happened under the Roosevelt regime that I happen to know he didn't know, and after they'd happened he'd tell me. Serious things, too. He's *only* the President, I used to say, and I make the same statement today about Pope Paul. He's *only* the pope. Seriously, heads of organizations are not always to blame for the affairs of their organizations. Now take that silver-list thing. Sure, that hurt me at the time. I didn't even know about that investment until the list appeared. But when you're the head of an organization you've got to be a man and take responsibility.

Wasn't that about the time that a prominent congressman threatened to kick you from the Capitol to the White House in your clerical garb "with all the silver in your pockets"?

No, I think that was later—a couple of years later.

When you began your 1934–35 broadcast season in September you asked your listeners to write and tell you if they wanted you to continue criticizing the New Deal. The results of that private poll were never revealed.

Don't ask me something like that, because I can't remember. All I remember is that I was getting many millions of letters. I had enough to do keeping up with the approximately two hundred clerks I had handling all this correspondence. Don't forget, during all of this, my first function was still parish priest. Eventually I had seven assistant priests, as the Shrine grew over the years from the twenty-eight families I started with to the more than 3,500 we had when I retired. Even when the assistants came I was still the pastor, and I knew what my duties were. I kept my parlor hours in the evening, even during the most hectic periods, so that my parishioners could stop by and talk about whatever they wanted to talk about. You know, about 99 per cent of the marital problems that came up could be solved if I could just get one of them to laugh. My parlor hours, that's the only thing I really miss in retirement.

Well, the listener poll must have been satisfactory, because you went on attacking certain New Deal programs, particularly the contributions of the "Drain Trusters," as you called them. Then, on November 11, 1934, you announced the formation of the National Union for Social Justice, complete with a sixteen-point platform to accomplish the "ever-elusive ideal of social justice" as spelled out in the papal encyclicals. Did you view this organization as a sort of people's lobby along the lines of the groups now headed by Ralph Nader and John Gardner?

Well, it was sort of an independent lobby. Really, at that time, I think I was a party man; I think that, whether or not I knew it, I was a Democrat, if you want to put it that way, whether or not I'd analyzed the whole meaning of the word democracy and all its implications. At any rate I was persuaded by a lot of gentlemen, important gentlemen around the country, to get up an organization for the purposes of indoctrinating the people with the principles of social justice. That was it. It wasn't political, although you can't prove it wasn't political. If you're indoctrinating anybody today, you're in politics.

At various times the National Union claimed as many as five million members. How many paying members did you have?

Nobody actually paid anything. What they did was buy the National Union's weekly newspaper, *Social Justice*. At its peak we had over 1,200,000 paid subscribers.

Without going all through the sixteen points would you briefly define the term "social justice"?

Well, there are two definitions of man. Man is a rational animal. That definition came all the way from Aristotle and Socrates and those people, who were animal nine-tenths of the time and rational one-tenth. But that doesn't tell the whole story. Man is a rational *social* animal, because, first of all, man is only a half a human being; the other half is a woman. No one is a complete totality. Secondly, no man is an island, as John Donne pointed out; no one is a Robinson Crusoe. Whatever each man's specialty is, he needs someone else to cut his hair, to grow his wheat, to sail his ships. To all, different gifts, see. We *need* one another. So social justice is a little bit different from personal justice. Social justice is the justice that one human being or one group of human beings should have toward another group of human beings, who make contributions to the well-being of total society, without which society itself would crumble.

The controversy begins when one tries to translate these general ideals into specific programs?

Yes, and how many dollars each gets.

In 1935 you became more and more critical of the Roosevelt administration.

I was very disappointed with the lack of genuine monetary reform, and I said so. And some of the relief programs just weren't working well, and I said so. And I told Mr. Roosevelt, too. As fine as Mr. Roosevelt was, he was a very poor businessman, one of the worst that ever sat in the White House. His own father, when writing his will, didn't leave him a nickel; he left the management of the estate in charge of somebody else, you know that, don't you? Well, I didn't blame Mr. Roosevelt for a lot of these policies. It was the fault of some of the men around him, but I couldn't go around being critical of his underlings. The President is the head of the organization and must take the responsibility.

D*o you still feel that way?*

I was pretty young. It was a young man's mistake, personalizing those attacks. I wouldn't stand for anyone attacking any President today. Since this upheaval against authority in the world today, I'm so fearful of these attacks on the President, I don't want to see his authority eroded.

Because of your huge following and your criticism of the New Deal, there was much speculation in 1935 about you and Senator Huey Long combining to form a third party. Was such a plan in the works?

All that speculation was absolutely false. I never discussed a third party with Long, or much of anything else, for that matter. I didn't know the senator that well. I met him several times in social situations, you know, with a bunch of senators or something. The only time I ever saw him alone was when he was sick in his Washington hotel, and Mrs. Garner, the wife of the Vice President, asked me to pay him a visit. We drove over in her car, and she waited outside while I went in.

May I ask what was discussed at that meeting?

Why, his health, of course. I was only in there about ten minutes. It was just a social call, and I wouldn't have gone at all if Mrs. Garner hadn't asked me to.

Was there one thing in particular, one issue or one incident, that caused you to break with the Roosevelt administration?

There was, but I can't talk about the specific details because there are some people living that can't stand this thing. But the fact was that some evidence had come to the attention of my bishop which indicated that certain officials in the Roosevelt administration were helping the Communist cause overseas. Well, Bishop Gallagher called me to his home one day, it was the summer of 1935, and he said, "Now, Charles, you're through supporting the New Deal and Mr. Roosevelt," and he showed me this evidence.

Did you take this evidence to the President?

I'm getting to that. You see, prior to this time, I had gotten quite close to Mr. Roosevelt through Joe Kennedy. We used to go down to his family home in Poughkeepsie— we always referred to it as Poughkeepsie, Hyde Park was a sort of dirty word—about every two weeks and visit Mr. Roosevelt. Well, after Michael Gallagher showed me this material I stopped going, and Mr. Roosevelt noticed that I seemed to be avoiding him, so one night, at the beginning of September, 1935, I got a call from Joe Kennedy to the effect that the "Boss" wanted to see me. I knew what it was all about, so I checked with my bishop, and he said it was all right to go.

The "Boss" was Mr. Roosevelt?

Yeah. So at any rate I got on a train and rode all night and finally got to Albany about four in the morning. As I got off the train a newsboy came up, shouting the headline about Huey Long's death. He had been shot a few days before, but he had just died. I bought a paper, and then Joe drove up in his Rolls Royce—he drove his own car in those days—and we drove back to Mr. Roosevelt's house. Well, there was nobody awake, of course, so we went up to a little kitchen and made ourselves some breakfast. I guess the President got up about six—he was always an early riser—and he called to us from the top of the stairs. You know, he really walked on his arms. He had the strongest arms and shoulders of any man I ever saw. Well, I ran up the stairs to lend him my shoulder, and I still had the morning newspaper under my arm. He noticed it, and I showed him the headline and said, "Hey, your boyfriend is dead." He got the news of Long's death from me.

What was the President's reaction?

He blanched. He was shocked. You see, he liked Huey Long. Lots of people did. Everybody liked his buffoonery, a special kind of buffoonery he had that caused people to laugh. It made people like him as a person, quite apart from his politics or philosophy.

What happened then?

We went down to the President's little breakfast nook and talked for a while, and finally he asked why I hadn't been around much. I sort of hemmed and hawed a bit, so finally he told Joe to "go look at the pigs"—he didn't have any pigs, of course; it was just a little joke he used to make. Joe laughed and went out, and then I showed the President the evidence that Michael Gallagher had received. We talked for six hours that day.

What did the President say about it?

He just kept saying, "It can't be true" and "I don't believe it." I told him that his plan to recognize Russia diplomatically and to extend credit to the Soviets was all right, because it was obvious that no nation could go bankrupt without affecting all the other nations in the world. But this evidence, the evidence I showed him, this was just too much.

Did the President ever look into the matter?

I don't really know. What I gave him was a copy of a public document, and I told him, when you get back to Washington, you have the ways and means of finding out the truth of the matter. But it was never mentioned again.

Did you part friends?

He wanted Joe and me to stay for dinner, but we had already made plans to drive up to the home of a friend of ours in Great Barrington. On the way up I told Joe most of the story, and when we got there Kennedy asked the butler to bring him some writing paper, and he sat down —I remember he pushed some dishes aside, the table had been set for dinner—and wrote out his resignation as chairman of the SEC.

That was on September 10, 1935?

It was the day after Huey Long died, yes.

And that fall you announced a "hunting season" on Congress, meaning that your National Union for Social Justice was going to become involved in the Congressional primaries the next year.

Yes.

The candidates endorsed by the National Union won twelve of twenty-four contests in Pennsylvania and thirteen of eighteen in

Ohio. Did you consider this part of the struggle for social and economic reform that you had hoped would be undertaken by the Roosevelt administration?

That's right. We tried to get it through the House; that was the aim, but it didn't work.

On June 19, 1936, you abruptly announced to your listeners the formation of a Union Party ticket headed by Representative William Lemke of North Dakota. "It is not pleasant for me who coined the phrase 'Roosevelt or ruin'—a phrase based upon promises—to voice such passionate words," you explained. "But I am constrained to admit that 'Roosevelt and ruin' is the order of the day because the moneychangers have not been driven from the temple." How do you feel about that campaign today?

It was a horrible mistake. I was persuaded to do that by a lot of nincompoops.

Why do you say that?

That was no way to indoctrinate people.

Did you consult with the other officials of the National Union for Social Justice before you nominated "Liberty Bill" Lemke?

No, no one was consulted. I think it was a meeting with Lemke one day, either in New York or here, and I said, "You'd make a pretty good President yourself. You've got the right ideas about finance and the right ideas about farming." We had, who was this boy, [Secretary of Agriculture Henry] Wallace, I think, pontificating about agriculture and those things at that time, see. I guess he was a theorist. So I said to Lemke, "At least, you'd make a pretty good farmer-President." But the campaign was a horrible mistake.

For the Union Party effort you joined forces with the California old-age-pension advocate, Dr. Francis Townsend, and Gerald L. K. Smith, who had succeeded the late Huey Long as leader of the Share-Our-Wealth movement.

I was supposed to be an associate of Townsend and Smith. I met Townsend once in my life for about five minutes in Cleveland and Smith for about three minutes before the same rally. I didn't know anything about him. Same with Townsend. That was the thing then, for these persons to attach themselves to you, and then do something to defame you.

The Cleveland rally you mentioned, that was the Townsendite convention in mid-July at which you dramatically took off your coat and clerical collar and brought the ten thousand people in the audience to their feet by denouncing "Franklin Double-crossing Roosevelt" as a "liar" and "a great betrayer." Your gesture with the collar, was that for oratorical effect?

It was about 105 degrees in the shade.

Did you regret having called the President a liar?

Yes, yes, yes, yes, and I said so publicly.

Your bishop, Michael Gallagher, was en route at that time to visit Pius XI. The New York Times quoted him, on July 27, to the effect that his trip to Rome had nothing to do with your political activities. What was the purpose of his trip?

To discuss me—favorably. He and Bishop Schrembs went together. But he couldn't afford to tell state secrets to the reporters like that.

But when Bishop Gallagher returned to this country he told the press that he considered Roosevelt the best candidate.

So did I.

You did? Can I ask you a personal question? Whom did you vote for in 1936?

I couldn't tell you now. I really can't remember.

On October 8, 1936, Eugenio Cardinal Pacelli, the Papal Secretary of State and subsequently Pius XII, came to the United States. The purpose of his extended tour was never announced, but his arrival started the press speculating that he was investigating you.

Cardinal Pacelli was no friend of mine, no friend of Michael Gallagher's. When he came over to discuss me with Mr. Roosevelt he came out to have a meeting of the bishops in Cleveland. So, all the bishops had to appear at this meeting, and Pacelli, well, he wouldn't talk to either Michael Gallagher or Joe Schrembs. He scorned them. So the bishop came back and he said, "Boy, have I got news for you. You're finished." And when Pius XI died in 1939, I was.

Were you worried when you learned that the Papal Secretary of State was, as you put it, "no friend" of yours?

No, I was weary. You can get weary doing this sort of thing. You get tired. You wish you lived in Portugal for about six months. To get away from it.

The 1936 Presidential campaign had more than its share of vitu-

peration. According to my notes, even your friend Joe Kennedy turned against you and called you a disgrace to the cloth.

Joe said that? Oh, no, no, no. Whoever quoted him as saying that just isn't telling the truth. No, that's not true. Of course the ACLU [American Civil Liberties Union] and that group down there, who I think came next door to hating me, they'd say anything to harm me.

I'm sorry, I was wrong. That quote was attributed to John B. Kelly, the Democratic chairman of Philadelphia.

I knew it wasn't Joe Kennedy. He wouldn't have said such a thing. Not that we always agreed on everything. Sometimes he'd tell me I was a jackass, but he'd never call me a disgrace.

In the course of your career you were called everything from a demagogue to a Fascist to an anti-Semite. How did these accusations affect you?

It never bothered me. I've often tried to analyze that psychologically. It hurt for the time being, for the first ten minutes. It's different when you're married, you have to take those things into consideration because of your wife and family. When you're unmarried it doesn't bother you. I'm talking psychologically. It's water on a duck's back, as it were. And because you're not seeking money, and it doesn't affect your pocketbook, that's the second reason. And thirdly, and it's the major reason, it's a gross untruth, and any day I wanted to, I could pull the strings from under them.

One of the high-water marks of the Union Party's 1936 campaign was a rally that drew forty-two thousand people to Cleveland's Municipal Stadium on August 16, 1936. Just before you collapsed from heat prostration you stated that you would quit the radio if Lemke didn't receive at least nine million votes.

I wish I had collapsed sooner. It was a rash promise.

Lemke didn't receive a million votes.

Why, he didn't even get 900,000. The whole thing was a horrible mistake. I was glad when it was over.

Did the campaign end your relationship with Roosevelt?

Oh, no. I continued to see him until the war started, not as frequently, of course. But you see, I genuinely liked the man, and I think he enjoyed me. His wife didn't.

Do you want to talk about Eleanor Roosevelt?

No, that's not fair. She leaned too far to the left to suit me, that's all.

Despite your campaign promise, you returned to the airwaves in 1937, but things were never the same again, were they?

Not after the death [January 20, 1937] of Bishop Gallagher, no. I was very close to Michael Gallagher. I loved that man. He was probably one of the great theologians in the country.

You didn't enjoy the same type of relationship with his successor, Archbishop Edward Mooney?

I'll tell you the story about that, but there is one thing you have to remember: Bishop Mooney was a real gentleman, a good gentleman. Well, years before—Michael Gallagher told me this—years before, Mooney had been the president of the Cleveland Latin School, and Joe Schrembs was the bishop there. Now in those days Michael was a Sinn Feiner, as most of the Irish bishops were, and he was invited down to Cleveland by the local Sinn Fein society to make a speech. And when he got there, his throat hurt so much he couldn't talk. So he told Bishop Schrembs about his problem, and Schrembs told him not to worry, he'd get someone to read it for him. So Schrembs called in Father Mooney and asked him to deliver the speech, and Mooney refused. He told Schrembs that he didn't believe in Sinn Fein. "What," said Schrembs, "you're an Irishman, and you don't believe in freedom for Ireland? Then get out of my diocese." And he suspended Mooney on the spot. Well, Mooney had powerful friends, and he eventually made his way to the American College in Rome, where he was consecrated a bishop. Well, he became archbishop after Michael Gallagher died, and one day he had me downtown to discuss something with me, 'twasn't very pleasant. I said, "Bishop, let's get this thing straight. You are here to be the hatchet-man for Pius XII, and I want you to do the job, because I stand back of him, if he told me to jump off this window. Don't be afraid. I hold no animosity toward you. You're doing your job, and I stand back of authority." There were tears in his eyes. He didn't have much courage, he didn't have much fortitude, but he was a gentleman.

Mooney wanted you to submit your radio scripts for review, didn't he?

He did it in a clumsy way. He appointed nine young priests who supervised my script on a Wednesday evening prior to the Sunday broadcast. And the nine of them, I don't know if any of them knew anything about political economy. I told Mooney, I'm not disclaiming their intelligence, but they haven't had enough experience. I knew it wasn't going to last.

In the late 1930's you became increasingly isolationist in your foreign-policy statements on the radio and in your weekly newspaper, Social Justice.

As I said, my generation considered the next world war a foregone conclusion after the Treaty of Versailles. I was most interested in stopping World War II; Mr. Roosevelt wasn't. He thought that this had to be done. He had been sold a package that Nazism was the most damnable thing on the face of the earth, and therefore, if he joined Communism to fight Nazism, it would be all right to get rid of it. And I was trying to sell the proposition that, now don't distinguish between the two of them too much. Marxism is the word you've got to get in your vocabulary. Nazism is only the left wing, Communism is only the right wing [*sic*] of the same bird of prey. Let them fight it out between themselves, and afterward we'll all go in for the kill. I still think I was right.

Did you consider yourself an isolationist?

An isolationist? No, I was the same as Mr. Hoover, I was the same as Charles Lindbergh, I was the same as a hundred other prominent Americans I could mention who weren't being attacked because they weren't getting publicity. I didn't want anybody to help Russia or Germany. I wanted them to fight it out themselves. Because I still have hope that Russia will come back to Christianity, will come back to normalcy. But because I came right out and said this, I was accused of being pro-Germany. How could I have been for this pup Hitler? There was never anything worse in the mystical body of Satan than this fellow Hitler.

Others accused you of being an Anglophobe.

No I'm not! Some of my best friends live over in Essex and Sussex in England. I've been against some of the English government over there, but if you can't be against a political party without being anti the whole country, what's wrong?

But after the war started in 1939, to be against the British government was widely interpreted in this country as being pro-German, wasn't it?

Well, now, there were some Jews in this country that

started this, especially the ACLU people. At that time the Jews were all for aid to Russia, don't forget, and I wasn't going for that, so to minimize my effect on that, they said I was anti-Semite. That was always a good ploy. This thing about my being pro-German, I was just as much against the Nazis, because I knew well enough that Nazi was a bad word, Communist was a bad word, Mussolini's Fascist was a bad word. The right word was Marxist. I've always used the generic word, Marxist. We're getting a form of Marxism in this country here. I don't know what they're going to call it. They're not going to call it Communism or Nazism, but one day they'll wake up and coin a name for it here. All the Marxist principles are here now, materialism, materialistic concept of life, and all this sort of stuff. It's in the works.

*W*hat about the charge that you are anti-Semitic?

I'm certainly not against the Jews. After all, Christ, if he's got any blood in his veins, was a Jew. And he has Mary's blood in his veins, anyway, we Catholics believe. He was conceived by the Holy Ghost, but he has Mary's blood in his veins. The Twelve Apostles were Jews, and I would say—it might shock you to hear this—that of all the popes we've had, about 30 per cent were Jews, with Jewish blood in their veins. There's nothing wrong with the Jews, any more than there's anything wrong with the Irish. I always resented the use of the term anti-Semitic because, after all, the Jews are only a very small portion of the Semite race, the smallest, in fact. So I'm not anti-Semitic. I am anti some Jews. Some of the international bankers I attacked were Jews, but I attacked them, not because they were Jews, but because they were international bankers who took good American money that should have been invested in this country and used it to set up the revolution in Russia in 1917. I'm certainly anti-ACLU for all the dirty things they do all the time. They're never on the right side of the decent Jewish things, even. My Jewish friends are against them. They think they're the shanty Irish of their race. But the minute I talk about a Jew who happens to be a misdemeanor Jew, therefore I'm anti-Semite. That's not . . . I've talked about more Irishmen. I'm not anti-Irish.

Would you describe yourself as anti-Zionist?

I'm not anti-Zionist, but I don't go for them. These Zionists aren't well-liked people anywhere. They're like the I.R.A. [Irish Republican Army] over in Ireland. They're not nice things to bring up, but you can't throw an umbrella over a whole nationality and say that there are no buncos in that nationality.

I asked that because in July, 1938, Social Justice published the now discredited Protocols of the Elders of Zion, which was alleged to give details of a centuries-old Jewish conspiracy to control the world.

How I came in touch with these *Protocols* to begin with, don't ask me. I must have had two hundred copies of them sent to me from all over the world. I had them in every language. Why? I don't know. Who told them to send them? I don't know. I was on the air, and I was a popular character, that's about all. I got them, and I think I've read everything about the *Protocols*, and I think I've studied them as much as any living American my age. First of all, I don't know the certain truth about them; I don't think anybody does. I couldn't prove they're false, I couldn't prove they're genuine.

You said in your introduction to the Protocols *in the newspaper that it wasn't important whether or not they were genuine, only that the Zionists should disavow them.*

Yes, but as I said, nobody knows the certain truth about them. How old the *Protocols* are, I can't get back farther than the sixteenth century, for sure. Who circulated them first, I don't know. But it's such a mystery, and there's such contradictions to it, that the safest thing to do about the *Protocols* is forget you ever read them, and try to be a Christian for ten minutes, because the Christian attitude toward all these things, even toward Communism, and there's no doubt who wrote the *Manifesto*, is this: Father, forgive them, for they know not what they do.

There seems to be some confusion about your exact relationship with Social Justice. *Did you actually control the newspaper?*

You mean financially? Yes, I did financially.

No, I meant editorial control.

I'm supposed to have, but there were some weeks when I was away. I wasn't even there to be consulted about what was going in the paper. But it was in my name, and when we were attacked for doing this and doing that and the other thing, because I was the publisher—sure, it's mine. That's the only way a man could do. There were many, many things that appeared in *Social Justice* that I wouldn't know anything about until maybe two or three weeks afterward.

Some people considered the newspaper a scurrilous publication for doing such things as printing a pink-tinted photograph of Eleanor Roosevelt. Did you know about that before it appeared?

No, no, I didn't.

On October 21, 1939, the paper demanded the impeachment of President Roosevelt. Did you have a hand in this?

I had none. But what's the use of saying I didn't have any hand in it? I was the owner of *Social Justice*. I was the publisher of *Social Justice*.

Were you ever concerned about the enormous influence you seemed to have over your audience? How did this power affect you?

I thoroughly believed in what I was doing, and I tried to be honest. I've spent my whole life defending the things I believed in. And I've always been loyal to my country. I'd die for it. That's not poetry with me. I've never forgotten Cardinal Mercier's old statement that he who lacks patriotism can never say he loves God. You've got to love your country, but love doesn't mean you have to be full of adulation. You have to love it and try to correct the wrongs.

As your views on the approaching war became more and more *controversial some of the radio stations on your network, like* WOR *in New York, began finding excuses to drop your program. Then, late in 1939 the National Association of Broadcasters adopted a new code that prohibited the sale of air time to "controversial" speakers. You were the primary target of the code. Was this what finally ended your radio career?*

They used that instrumentality, too. But what really put me off the air was the committee of young priests that Mooney established to censor my broadcasts. It became an impossibility to carry on. One of the priests told me once that they would take a pencil and just indiscriminately knock a page out. At one point I was writing enough for four hours of air time so they'd have something to take out. So finally it got down to the point where I called up Archbishop Mooney, and I said, "Archbishop, I want you to know, you've got down to the point now where I can't get up and recite the last half of the Hail Mary." So I said to him, "Come on right out and say so." And he said, "No, I can't. They won't let me say so. They want you to quit." "Oh," I said, "they do. That's the first time you told me. Fine. I'm through."

By "they" did he mean the review committee?

No, Rome. Pius XII was no friend of mine.

Were there any hard feelings between you and Mooney?

Of course not. He used to come out to the Shrine once and a while, for confirmations or something like that. When he came out he was always gracious, and I always received him graciously, and I always had a bottle of his favorite Bristol Cream, and we always had a drink together. In fact, during his last illness, in the last year and a half of his life, I was one of the few persons who used to go down and see him. He knew that I was, of all things, an obedient priest.

The final act, in a sense, occurred in March, 1942, when U.S. Attorney General Francis Biddle, presumably at the urging of President Roosevelt, asked the Post Office to "suspend or revoke" the second-class mailing privilege of Social Justice *and ordered a federal grand jury investigation.*

That was a horrible thing. They came up to the Shrine with Army trucks and took all my files away, a million names of the mailing list, all the papers and the letters, wagonload after wagonload, and I've never received them back. I guess they junked them in Washington someplace. And they took about twelve of my secretaries down to Washington. I challenged them publicly, "Bring me down and ask me the questions." And they wouldn't accept it. Why they had these lip readers in the dining rooms down there, and my secretaries would go to dinner, and they'd tell them the next day in court what they said at dinner. I was supposed to have been on the side of the Nazis, I was supposed to have gone to Germany, I was supposed to have seen Hitler. All nonsense.

Biddle wrote later that the administration was trying to avoid putting a priest on trial for sedition.

Biddle couldn't have tried me for anything. If Biddle had ever tried me for sedition, *he* would have been tried for a lot of other things, because I had attorneys stronger and smarter than Biddle. He knew perfectly well that if he had ever tried me, a case would be brought against him personally that would have put him in limbo forever.

That's no way to fight. Those young girls didn't know anything about me. Bring me down there, and put the questions to me. I'll ánswer any question truthfully. But Biddle was only doing as he was instructed to do, we don't know by whom.

You don't think Roosevelt knew about it?

He knew about it to begin with, yes.

My understanding is that Biddle finally sent an emissary, a man named Leo Crowley, to talk to Archbishop Mooney, who then called you in on May 1, 1942, and threatened defrockment unless you agreed to be silent for the duration of the war.

No, no, no. There's no truth in that. Mooney and I were good friends all the way through. And I never heard of Crowley in my life till the whole thing was over. He certainly never saw me. You know, you can't condemn a man without giving him a hearing, which they never gave me. But they didn't want to give me a hearing. They just wanted to smear me.

Did you meet the archbishop on May 1?

No. There was no confrontation of any kind.

How did you feel when the public part of your career ended at that time?

I felt relieved.

In retrospect, Father, what do you consider your finest accomplishments?

First of all, I was the first man in the clergy to bring social justice to the minds of the public, even to indoctrinate them that such a thing existed. And in doing so, I was the first man of the cloth to let them know that the clergy has a duty, not a right, to do this.

Would you consider yourself to have been in the vanguard of today's activist clergy, and what is your opinion of them?

Well, I'm a priest, and I certainly was an activist. Today's activists? Some of them are wonderful; some of them I don't agree with. I certainly can't go along with the destruction of property. I don't believe in going to these barbaric excesses. You see, you can't have disorder to get your point across. There are two things you can't throw aside when you're in public life. You must be a gentleman. Once in a while you slip, as I've done myself. And always you must be a Christian, and remember that you're not representing yourself, you're representing your church.

Is there a specific accomplishment that you take special pride in?

There are dozens of things, some of them probably more important to me than they would be to the public. But what about unionism? Don't forget that the UAW [United Auto Workers] was started in my kitchen down at the Shrine of the Little Flower. The early leaders of that union used to meet with me for breakfast each Sunday after the nine o'clock Mass, and we'd talk about it. They didn't have a strong enough organization, and I was trying to teach them to fight politically.

The UAW presents social justice awards every year. Is this your influence?

Oh, sure. I spent many an hour and many thousands of dollars helping get that thing going.

Henry Ford was a friend of yours. How did he react to your efforts to organize the auto workers?

Henry Ford was all for it. He was only afraid that the wrong people would get control. "Get the wrong people, they'll turn it on me," he used to say. "Get the right people, they'll work with me."

Yet at the end of his life, Henry Ford was identified as an archfoe of organized labor.

Oh, yes. He was "anti-Semite," he was "antiunion," he was "a selfish old moneybags." People didn't know Henry Ford. There are so many people maligned. When you get to be my age, you look back at so many people who were maligned. It's so easy to condemn when you don't know the circumstances. And so many lies get themselves written down as gospel truth. And another thing. When you get to be my age, you don't really care any more. I mean, what's the use of contradicting them?

Father, one last question. If you had your life to live over again, is there anything you would do differently?

There is nothing I would do the same.

Robert S. Gallagher, formerly a staff editor, has recently rejoined us as a contributing editor. He is at work on a biography of the famous congressman Thomas "Czar" Reed (1839–1902).

ANSWERS TO "EARLY AMERICAN IMPLEMENTS"

1. Ice axe.
2. Post axe, used for cutting mortises in beams.
3. Lard squeezer.
4. Armrest, often used during long church meetings.
5. Feather-bed patter, used for smoothing out feather mattresses and quilts.
6. Wheel race, used for measuring the circumference of a wheel before fitting it with its metal rim.
7. Candlemaker. Wicks were tied to it and dipped into hot wax.
8. Leather, or beaming, knife, used for dressing hides.
9. Hay saw.
10. Screw, used for loosening sugar in a sugar barrel.
11. Wheelwright's reamer, used for boring hub holes.
12. Froe, used for splitting wood into shingles.
13. Round shave, or scorper, used to smooth the inside of a barrel and also to make bowls of wood.
14. Hook pins, or drift hooks, used to peg beams together temporarily when laying a framework on the ground, before raising a house.

Reading, Writing, and History

We are still seeing slavery through a glass, darkly, and small wonder. For the legacy of race conflict, slavery's deformed child (or perhaps its parent), remains with us, refusing to be banished by all our piety and wit.

We would like to turn our eyes away from it, but we cannot. All we can do is try to see both past and present clearly, hoping that intelligence will make us free of anger and error and find a way to a peaceable future. The quest for the historical truth of slavery is therefore a cleansing and valuable task. When that task is shared by historians of both races, whose goal is to unveil the reality of the past and not necessarily to confirm anyone's prejudices (black or white, liberal or conservative), there is cause for rejoicing among professional historians and their readers. Academic training has some use, after all; it cuts across lines of bias and conditioning in a helpful way.

Consider two books. *American Counterpoint* is the work of a distinguished white history professor at Yale, who is now over sixty years of age—and who was born in Arkansas. It appeared in 1971. A year later John Blassingame —also a Yale faculty historian— emerges with his study, *The Slave Community*. Blassingame is a Southerner by birth, too. But he is thirty-two years younger than Woodward, and

110

AMERICAN COUNTERPOINT:
*Slavery and Racism in the
North-South Dialogue,
by C. Vann Woodward.*
Little, Brown and Co., 301 pp. $7.95

THE SLAVE COMMUNITY:
*Plantation Life in the
Antebellum South,
by John W. Blassingame.*
Oxford Univ. Press, 272 pp. $7.95

black. Yet somehow, without planning, one is sure, both books take a sharp view of some legends that have grown up around the "peculiar institution." Both uncompromisingly assail the actual record with piercing questions. And both men wind up with studies that defy some of our prejudices, prod us with yet unanswered questions, and somehow make us feel that we have moved a little closer to liberating truth.

Consider, now, just a few of the ideas about slavery and the black race that have been current (and often in conflict) in historical circles for the last dozen years or so:

—Blacks were stripped of their language, religion, customs, and culture in slavery and taught just enough of their masters' ways to make them

By BERNARD A. WEISBERGER

tractable. They were denied family life, rendering their menfolk especially irresponsible since they could not protect their own children. Some slaves responded to this cultural rape by adopting a "Sambo" personality —childlike, undisciplined, humorous, and dependent.

—Blacks *pretended* to acquiescence in slavery and affection for their white plantation owners and neighbors but actually were filled with rebelliousness.

—Slaves suffered more in white, Protestant America than in the colonies of Catholic Spain, France, and Portugal. This was because the American slave was simply a piece of capital goods in a liberal society that let each planter do what he liked with his property; whereas in the Latin colonies the royal government intervened to guarantee that the king's wards got some protection, and the Church had a hand in seeing that the pope's flocks were educated in their Christian duties. Moreover, Anglo-Saxons worried more about racial purity than Frenchmen or Spaniards and made no legal distinction between the coal-black Negro and the octoroon. In Latin America, by contrast, there was more recognition accorded to mulattos and a rising scale of privileges that went with each degree of lightness.

To say in detail what these books do to such assumptions is impossible in a short space. It is worthwhile, however, to point out a brace of the generalizations to which Woodward pays close and fruitful attention. To begin with, there is the matter of slave numbers and mortality. Woodward, relying on the best and latest scholarship, dismisses exaggerated claims that perhaps forty million Africans were shipped out (after first being enslaved by other Africans!) during the trade's macabre centuries of life. He finds the count closer to ten million, and of these, only about 450,000 came to England's North American colonies. Yet those 450,000 had swelled to four million by the time of the Civil War, whereas in supposedly less harsh Latin America the slave populations not only did not increase but actually declined by as much as half in the same period. This, Woodward notes, should give us pause in our assessment. Did American planters simply take better care of their "stock"? Did they encourage larger numbers of their black women to "breed"? (That charge, levelled by abolitionists, was always denied by Southerners.) Or is there some Malthusian factor at work that we have not yet isolated?

Woodward also takes a sharp glance at the Brazilian plantation, which is somehow supposed to have followed a pattern that made the absorption of blacks easier, after emancipation, than it was in the United States. He finds it to have been tolerant of racial differences, indeed—tolerant in an almost Biblical way. In translation this means that for the Brazilian planters, polygamous miscegenation was an acceptable pattern. They had numerous slave mistresses, and they sustained their power to do so with an authoritarian sway over their households that reduced their white women also to virtual chattels dwelling among their husbands' concubines. And some Brazilian plantation patriarchs also were capable of savage punishments,

petulant rages, and drunken idleness on a scale that would have made Simon Legree look benign or Augustin St. Clare purposeful by contrast.

Blassingame, too, has myths to puncture. He notes, first of all, that the so-called extinction of African culture was far from complete. Long after shipment from Africa there were on the plantations musicians, drummers, singers, tellers of tales, carvers of wood in traditional forms, and conjurers who played important roles in the slave community. The "cultural rape" theory does not rest on sound evidence.

Moreover, a careful study of plantation records and of narratives composed by escaped slaves indicates that a kind of family and community structure endured in the quarters. Law or no law, many slave fathers did their best, even when it involved infrequent or difficult visits to neighboring plantations where their wives were located, to look after and set models for their children. Furthermore, within the world of field and cabin there were blacks whose special strength, skill, and cunning allowed them to master various crafts. These became indispensable to their owners, but in addition earned respect among the slaves themselves. The head blacksmith or cotton-gin mechanic, the black overseer—these were men who had to be won over before a job could be well done, as any master soon learned. And they were often the figures turned to by the slaves during crises, having earned that instinctive reliance that people place on natural leaders.

Finally, Blassingame notes, generalizations about slave personality skimp the actual complexity of plantation life. There were some "Sambos," indeed. There also were—as the records show—slaves who literally would not submit to punishment or intimidation. In between were those who knew when to push and when to yield, when to shirk and when to hustle, which white folks could be

handled and which could not. There were slaves easily broken by punishment, and others manageable only by those whom they could respect or love. The documents indicate, in fact, that people are people even under the extreme stresses of a system as outrageous to our modern ideas of human dignity as slavery.

For after all, to say that many blacks lived lives of occasional satisfaction and pride, even in bondage, is not to say that they were debased or docile, but simply that they had tremendous capacity to endure. The human animal's persistence in asserting personality in the face of crushing disaster is amazing. The observation that some kind of slave society remained intact under the shadow of the lash is not inconsistent with the reality of occasional black rebellion or perennial black craving for freedom. It simply underscores the toughness of the slaves' spirit.

Both these writers know that they do not have the final truth of slavery. Both recognize that as an impossible goal, given an imperfect record and the fallibility of human nature. Blassingame writes: "The slave, like the master, gave *his* view of the institution. Both distorted reality as they viewed the world through their respective lenses." And Woodward notes that perhaps it would have been better for future peace between the races if Anglo-American masters had shared certain experiences (such as a past occupation by Moors) with those of Iberian background. "But then," he says, "that would have been somebody else's history and not our own." We must see both sides—indeed, all sides—of our history and accept the unchangeable reality of what we see. It might indeed be splendid if we had behaved like other peoples (or vice versa), but the moving finger has writ, and we have better uses for our energies than wishfully thinking it may be lured back to cancel half a line. That lesson alone may be one of the best to be derived from the study of history.

EARLY AMERICAN IMPLEMENTS:
WHAT ARE THEY?

Eric Sloane

ANSWERS ON PAGE 109